INTEGRATED STUDIES

Challenges to the College Curriculum

Edited by
Stephen H.

Preface by
James M. Banner, Jr.
Introduction by
Theodore L. Gross

UNIVERSITY
PRESS OF
AMERICA

KIRTLEY LIBRARY
COLUMBIA COLLEGE
COLUMBIA, MO 65216

Copyright © 1982 by
University Press of America, Inc.
P.O. Box 19101, Washington, D.C. 20036

All rights reserved
Printed in the United States of America

Library of Congress Cataloging in Publication Data
Main entry under title:

Integrated studies.

  Bibliography: p.
  Contents: The Ph. D. program in the humanities / Leon Golden -- The Master of Arts in humanities / Bettie Anne Doebler -- Interdisciplinary education at an upper division college / William J. Mahar -- [etc.]
  1. Universities and colleges--United States--Curricula--Addresses, essays, lectures. 2. Education, Humanistic--United States--Curricula--Addresses, essays, lectures. I. Dill, Stephen H.
LB2361.5.I57   1982   378'.1998'0973   82-17511

ISBN 0-8191-2794-9
ISBN 0-8191-2795-7 (pbk.)

This book is dedicated to Dr. Winberg Chai
who appreciates the importance of integrative studies.

iv

ACKNOWLEDGEMENTS

Material for the Selected Bibliography, pp. 133-142, from the CIJE database used by permission of the publisher, the Oryx Press, Phoenix, Arizona.

The editor wishes to thank Dr. Joseph Cash, Dean of the College of Arts and Sciences, the University of South Dakota, for providing both time and money for the preparation of this book; Sally Wheelock and Terri Bruyer for expert and efficient typing; and Jean Dill for the exacting task of proofreading.

Vermillion
August, 1982

vi

CONTENTS

Page

Preface, James M. Banner, Jr. ix
 American Association for the Advancement
 of the Humanities

Introduction, Theodore L. Gross xiii
 Pennsylvania State University, Capitol Campus

The Ph.D. Program in the Humanities 1
 Florida State University, Leon Golden

The Master of Arts in Humanities. 15
 Arizona State University, Bettie Anne Doebler

Interdisciplinary Education at an Upper Division
 College. 33
 Pennsylvania State University, Capitol Campus,
 William J. Mahar

Integrated Liberal Studies Program. 63
 University of Wisconsin, Madison, Michael
 Hinden

Humanities on the Border: A Special Interdisciplinary Program for a Unique Locale. 85
 University of Texas at El Paso, John Haddox

Integrated Humanities Program 107
 University of South Dakota, Stephen H. Dill

Extended Teacher Institutes 125
 University of South Dakota, Gale Crouse

Selected Bibliography 133
 University of South Dakota, Frank R.
 Cunningham and Susan J. Wolfe

viii

PREFACE

In a modern society as complex as that of the
United States, the structure and content of the college
curriculum is bound always to be debated. As society
and culture, the economy, and the nation's international
role change, so the methods and subjects by which citizens
are educated will change, too--as they have since
the earliest days of the republic. The college curriculum
has always mirrored society's aspirations for
its young and its view of its own future. It should
therefore occasion no surprise that, in an era as vexed
and confusing as ours, efforts to examine and alter
college education have become intensive again.

Although no standard college curriculum still
exists, critics of course offerings abound, most of
them either seeing irrelevant conformity or wholesale
abandonment of any curricular principles at all. Yet
if one listens to the criticisms--too much emphasis on
the classics, vocationalism run wild, the absence of a
core of courses, out-of-date confidence in the continuity
of knowledge, an elective system without rationale,
requirements filled with useless knowledge and impractical
culture--one hears as much incoherence as is
charged from all quarters against the curriculum itself.
For those who would try to alter the curriculum, some
cautions therefore seem appropriate: be specific in
criticism; claim no universal applicability for "reforms";
consider each curriculum in the context of its
own institution; accept variety among approaches; and
assume that no "solution", however satisfactory, is
timeless.

These cautions animate the essays collected in
this volume. The authors review programs designed to
address a single problem: the fragmentation of the
college curriculum. They report on local initiatives,
tailored to the diversity of history and mission of
individual institutions, and do not assume the existence
of one way to curricular integrity. They record
the compromises and flexibility essential to fashioning
reformed curricula whose shared, central aim is the
integration of learning.

The integration of knowledge has governed educational
thought since classical times and has remained
one of the cardinal goals of liberal education. Yet
the attainment of the goal has always been problematic,
never more so than today. Rather than the corrosive

ix

influence of the elective system or the growth and specialization of the professoriate, the fragmentation of knowledge itself seems to bar the way to genuine curricular integration. And few are the people, save those who would be arbitrary, who believe that in our lifetime knowledge will again possess the coherence it had, or appeared to have, a century or more ago.

What seems instead to be the goal of the efforts recorded here is to fashion a course of study, available to those who would take it, that centers on a general theme that is approached from a broad range of disciplinary perspectives. Whether that theme be intellectual and classic, such as the humanities, or cultural and modern, such as border state society; whether it be a B.A., M.A. or Ph.D. program; whether the students be undergraduates or teachers; the programs strive to hold students' attention upon the bonds of existence, the links between ideas, the interpretation of disciplines and specialties. In some cases the results have been uncertain, and manifest difficulties have attended each program. And yet all have been at least modestly successful, and some have achieved the result their initiators originally sought.

These essays help establish a permanent record of the origins, structure, and growth of distinctive curricular departures of the early 1980s. They are likely to be read as much for what they portray of contemporary intellectual currents. Surely, it has proven difficult to keep interdisciplinary programs alive when they cross departmental lines. Core courses, though not the emblem of interdisciplinary programs, have been maintained with difficulty. Similarly, obstacles posed by the structure, governance, and incentive and reward systems of the modern university have frequently forced adjustments in the faculty's aims. In each instance, however, the faculty has been flexible; has tried to marry grand intellectual ends with current student fashion, such as vocationalism; and has prepared itself to adjust course contents and subjects to faculty interests.

Whether the successes recorded here are typical of interdisciplinary initiatives elsewhere and how they will fare under increasingly confused academic conditions remains to be seen. It may be worth a retrospective look at them after a decade has passed. It should suffice here that we have in these essays a record both of admirable academic leadership at a time when it is

in short supply and of cautious experimentation governed
by the most venerable of educational purposes.

James M. Banner, Jr.
American Association for the
Advancement of the Humani-
ties

xii

INTRODUCTION

The title of this volume, "Integrated Studies: Challenges to the College Curriculum," expresses the fundamental problem confronting American education. In an age of intense concentration on vocational training and confusion as to the long-range significance of the humanities, the need for integrated studies is greater than ever before.

The problems that the college student will confront during his life time stem directly from a breakdown of cultural integration domestically and internationally. At home, we see that traditional institutions like the family, church, and school--once the collective center that defined values for most Americans--have lost much of their influence upon the morals of young people. Internationally, we live with the persistent outbreak of war and the threat of war.

In recent years we have underrated higher education because it has not proved to be the panacea we once hoped it would be. The enormous expansion of community colleges, colleges, and universities during the past twenty-five years has been attended by an expanding economy that has contributed to a sense of great expectations--from reforming social ills domestically to advancing democracy in other nations. These expectations have now diminished dramatically, as we regard some of the major events that have occurred since the early 1960's: the assassination of American leaders, the unleashing of nuclear energy, racial violence, student revolts, the Vietnam War, Watergate, the development of Petroleum Export Countries (OPEC), the taking of American hostages, the endless succession of dangerous Middle Eastern crises, rapid inflation, unemployment, and crime.

Clearly higher education cannot solve these problems alone. Surely a lesson of the sixties and seventies is that education can not resolve social and political and moral issues in the society at large--not by itself. But universities can have a deep impact on young people and must express a larger vision than merely meeting a momentary budget crisis. In addition to a broad curriculum, elective courses relating to world cultures and world affairs should be introduced; study abroad, resulting in a reading and speaking knowledge of a chosen language, must be encouraged; and faculty exchanges need to be sponsored. The only way such goals can be achieved is through integrated studies.

This volume touches upon the major administrative and curricular concerns involved with integrating the different disciplines of higher education. The essays by Leon Golden and Bettie Anne Doebler concentrate upon graduate work, which, of course, is the essential beginning since it serves as the guidepost for the rest of education. If graduate education remains as highly specialized as it has been in the past, future teachers can only perpetuate that attitude of mind as they teach at earlier levels of education. The models of The Florida State University and Arizona State University are worth examining closely. William Mahar's description of an interdisciplinary program at an upper division college--Penn State Capitol Campus--is an account of one of the most carefully organized and imaginative courses of study with which I am acquainted; it is particularly interesting because Capitol Campus draws upon students from different types of two-year institutions who bring different levels of educational preparation and background. Michael Hinden's account of a group of faculty redesigning the integrated liberal studies program at the University of Wisconsin/Madison reveals some of the practical problems associated with accommodating an interdisciplinary program in an institution where enrollments have diminished. John Haddox offers the interesting perspective of an "interdisciplinary border studies program" in which the El Paso campus at the University of Texas develops "a complementary character to the diverse cultures present in our communities." And, finally, scholar/teachers from the University of South Dakota--Stephen H. Dill, Gale Crouse, Frank Cunningham, and Susan Wolfe--close the volume through a series of essays that indicate how lively interdisciplinary studies are at that university. The selected, annotated bibliography is particularly useful for those who wish to pursue the subject further.

Education in the eighties must perform an integrative function for society and must stress clarity of expression, in writing and in speech. No discipline can exist in isolation any longer. The successful student nurse must know not only basic science but business management and health care law, and have a command of communications skills. The engineering student must be aware of the ethical implications of modern technology as well as the fundamental sciences, and he must have a command of communications skills.

The political science major needs this kind of comprehensive education and he certainly needs a command of communication skills. The student of humanities ought to know the principles and complexities of modern technology and, of course, possess communication skills. Beyond a fusion of disciplines, the common denominator for all of us is the ability to articulate the medium of knowledge, in writing and speech, with coherence and logic and clarity. In an age saturated by mass communicators, the accurate, forceful, and eloquent expression through language must be demanded by the university.

There is this constant pressure for easy answers that the university, more than any other force in American society, must resist. For all of its remarkable ability to concentrate upon the moment, television is not a medium sympathetic to ambiguity. Nor is print journalism. Nor government reports. An action-oriented, fragmented society whose deeds and misdeeds, great and trivial, are processed through the media without pause and with little deliberation, needs a place for reflection that will cherish the past; needs to create constructive ambiguity in the minds of students, young and old; needs to respond to change through continuing education without surrendering the accumulated wisdom of disciplines; and, most importantly, needs to provide the integrative function each of us, in and out of the university, craves. A troubled society needs a university to create the future.

Universities are not now integrative. Built upon discrete departments and disciplines, they have even found it difficult to agree upon a core curriculum, no less integrate one. But at the more advanced levels of education as well as the most elementary, integrating knowledge will be the great educational issue in the years remaining to this century. The experimental steps that lead toward integration can occur through continuing education and then be assimilated into the permanent disciplines--modifying them, reshaping them, with the deliberation and respect that great traditions deserve. The integration of knowledge may then become an integration of wisdom.

Wordsworth's famous sonnet too often defines our age:

The world is too much with us; late and soon,
Getting and spending, we lay waste our powers:
Little we see in Nature that is ours;

We have given our hearts away, a sordid boon!

This description need not be ours in the years to come; it need not be the epitaph of our age. If, as a society, we use our powers wisely, preserving culture as we adapt it to the times, we in the university will give society the direction it surely needs. We will help to create its future as well as preserve its past.

Stephen H. Dill has gathered together a most interesting collection of essays that should be of considerable practical use to classroom teachers.

Theodore L. Gross
Provost and Dean
Pennsylvania State University
Capitol Campus

THE PHD PROGRAM IN THE HUMANITIES
THE FLORIDA STATE UNIVERSITY

The evolution of the Ph.D. program in the Human-
ites at Florida State University has followed the essential guidelines set down for it at its inception as an
academic program in 1956. This interdisciplinary program has as its principal goal the provision of a distinctive, alternate approach to traditional ways of
training teachers in the field of higher education. At
the core of its program are two forms of integrated
studies; the first representing the articulation of a
variety of independent departmental offerings into a
unified program; and the second focussing on the development of core courses which in themselves represent an
integrating intellectual experience.

In order to understand the present status and goals
of this program something of its history and origins
must be related. Here I wish to quote from a report
written by the original director of this program which
clearly describes its genesis. The late Professor
Robert Miller of the Department of Philosophy wrote as
follows of the steps that led to the establishment of
the interdisciplinary doctoral program in the Humanities
at Florida State University:

Sometime during the 1953-1954 academic year Dr.
Milton Carothers, then Dean of the Graduate School,
called a special meeting of the Chairmen of the
several Humanities area departments. He raised the
question whether in the interests of the several
departments and in the interest of the relatively
new Florida State University Graduate School, the
departments might wish to consider the possibility
of developing an interdepartmental graduate program
leading to the Ph.D. in the Humanities. He cited
numerous discussions at meetings of graduate deans
which criticized the narrowness of many departmental Ph.D. programs, and which strongly recommended
broadening these programs both by the introduction
of interdisciplinary courses and by the introduction of new interdisciplinary programs. These
discussions with their criticisms and recommendations were paralleled by many articles in professional (Education and Administration) journals.
He also called attention to the fact that Syracuse
and Stanford Universities had recently introduced
and widely advertised such interdepartmental programs. Dr. Carothers asked these Humanities area

departmental representatives to consider whether
they might wish to consider broadening their offerings in either or both of these ways, and if they
did in fact wish to consider seriously this issue
to constitute themselves an Ad Hoc Committee on the
matter, to elect their own Chairman, and to report
to him whenever they might come to some decision--
either positive or negative. Without attempting to
influence the decision of the group, he did assert
that a positive decision would have his strong support. The representatives of the Humanities area
departments did agree to consider the matter, con-
stituted themselves an Ad Hoc Committee, and
elected R.D. Miller as Chairman. The Committee met
regularly, usually fortnightly, for a period of
nearly two years. It read the professional literature, studied the Syracuse, Stanford, and Chicago
interdepartmental programs, informally sampled
opinion of F.S.U. graduate students, and carefully
considered the recommendations included in the
Harvard Graduate Students Club study of the Harvard
graduate programs...The Committee in due time decided to recommend the introduction of a new graduate program leading to the Ph.D. in Humanities. In
proposing a new Ph.D. program the Committee explic-
itly or implicitly affirmed:
1. that the new interdepartmental program
   should be an independent clearly definable
   program admitting students directly;
2. that such a program would complement, not
   compete, with existing or yet to be developed departmental programs;
3. that the program should have a strong
   departmental orientation thus strengthen-
   ing the offerings of departments already
   approved to offer the Ph.D., and allowing
   departments not approved to offer the
   Ph.D. opportunity to expand and strengthen
   their graduate offerings;
4. that a minimum of specially designated
   Humanities courses be introduced;
5. that while interrelationships and integration be explored and developed in the
   specially designated (required or elective)
   Humanities courses, the most effective and
   significant interdisciplinary study would
   be developed by the student himself
   through the requirement that he take a
   cluster of courses from several departments
   focusing on a distinct cultural period or
   cultural movement;

6. that a program so conceived would provide a maximum of flexibility to allow almost any student to develop his special interests, yet be a controlled and identifiable program having most, if not all, of the traditional values of the doctoral program;
7. and that such a program would require a minimum of special funding.

The proposal was approved by Dean Carothers and F.S.U.'s Graduate Council. Late in the Spring of 1956, the proposal was approved by the Board of Control (now, Board of Regents). Without benefit of outside advertising the program officially began in September, 1956 with four students, all of whom had transferred to the program from departmental programs.

I would like now to discuss the major points listed above which represented the original conception of the interdisciplinary doctoral program in the Humanities and indicate how that original conception affects the program as it exists today. First, the program remains today, as it was when instituted, an independent doctoral program which admits students directly to graduate study. The director of the program remains the chief administrative officer of the program and the principal advisor to the students in the program. The director of the program is the only faculty member who currently has an officially recognized administrative assignment to the program and this constitutes one half of his professional commitment to the university, the other half being a departmental assignment. Within the past three years, however, an informal arrangement has been worked out so that an assistant director has been appointed who shares in the advising and administrative tasks that have grown considerably since the initiation of the program and an executive committee has been appointed which is available to give advice on policy matters to the director. Currently the executive committee consists of distinguished faculty members from the Departments of Religion, Philosophy, Art, Physics, and the School of Music. The director and the assistant director of the program are also members of the executive committee and their academic specializations are in the Departments of Classics and Modern Languages. Thus a structure has evolved for guiding the development of the program that is consistent with the rich interdisciplinary aspirations which were the basis of the origination of the program and which are still very much its principal justification for existence.

Since no one is assigned, for instructional purposes, directly to the program in the Humanities, all of those who teach in the program are faculty members who make a special request to do so and they represent the various departments which relate, in the broadest sense, to the Humanities. These faculty members teach the specially designated graduate courses and seminars which represent a unique dimension of the program and which we will describe in some detail below. Thus the program in the Humanities at Florida State University has a simple and easy to operate administrative structure which brings together, in a collegial atmosphere, a group of faculty members committed to interdisciplinary goals. Most of these faculty members are also individuals who have made significant contributions to their own disciplines and find the interdisciplinary opportunities afforded by the doctoral program in the Humanities complementary to, or in some way the fulfillment of, their disciplinary interests.

When the Ph.D. program in the Humanities was established at Florida State University it was stipulated that the program "complement, not compete, with existing or yet to be developed departmental programs." At the time of the inception of the program there were a number of Humanities departments or Humanities oriented departments which did not have doctoral programs of their own and which found a mechanism in the Humanities program for participating in doctoral level instruction. Thus at that time the potential for competition was minimal and the interdisciplinary Humanities program served the needs of a larger number of departments. Now, even though most departments have their own doctoral programs, we still have not found any significant problem of academic competition for faculty resources since no faculty members can be appointed directly to the program and all must be assigned to departments. Those faculty members who choose to teach in the interdisciplinary program do so with the full approval and support of a number of departments. The interdisciplinary program in the Humanities has been selected as one of the Humanities area departments and programs to be nominated for support through the Quality Improvement Program of the State of Florida which is designed to assist existing programs of strength to achieve national leadership and recognition. If these funds are made available to the program in the Humanities it will have new and very exciting resources at its disposal for achieving these goals.

The program draws students who have especially

4

selected it to meet their academic aspirations. As will be explained below all of these students have strong departmental training and have made a conscious decision to complete their academic work on an interdisciplinary basis. Thus there is not any divisive or abrasive competition for students. In an era of restricted opportunities for graduates in the field of the Humanities we are noting sustained and even increasing interest in our program. We find that we have a number of students entering our program to whom we were unable to make assistantship or fellowship awards, because of the limited number of such awards, but who are financing their graduate education through their own resources. We also note that a number of faculty members who hold teaching positions at various institutions, but who do not hold the doctorate, have selected our program in which to complete their academic work. We believe that this may result from the fact that in many institutions a faculty member may need to deal with more than one subject matter or discipline. In general, then, the interdisciplinary program in the Humanities has found strong departmental support here at Florida State University.

As has been mentioned when the doctoral program in the Humanities was instituted, a number of departments here did not have doctoral program of their own and made use of the interdisciplinary program in order to carry out graduate level instruction. Now that this no longer is the case, our program takes its essential justification from its interdisciplinary nature. It accomplishes its interdisciplinary goals in two ways: (1) through the establishment of a core of courses and seminars in the area of interdisciplinary Humanities and (2) through encouraging students to enroll in a variety of departmental courses that relate to a common theme.

It is expected that the student will make a synthesis of the ideas presented in the course work from the different departments. A typical student's program would involve the following components. First the student would be required to enter the program with an M.A. or its equivalent in one of the traditional Humanities disciplines. If the student did not have a degree of this type then the student could be admitted provisionally but would be required to take additional post M.A. work in that subject matter discipline or area in order to achieve a greater degree of professional control of that academic discipline. The student would then be required to choose a concentration in a major chronological period and to select courses from several appropriate departments in order to meet this requirement.

It is here that we would expect the student to make a personal synthesis of the courses chosen to represent the major period. The student would then have a choice in the next requirement that must be fulfilled. The student could select a minor chronological period and deal with it as with the major period only taking fewer hours in this area.

An increasingly popular alternative to the minor chronological period has been the choice of a Cultural Theme. Here the student can select such topics as "Existentialism" or "The Nature of Faith" and take concentrated work, often involving individualized instruction, dealing with this theme. Finally the student must fulfill two requirements involving interdisciplinary Humanities courses and seminars which will be described below.

When the program was established it was stipulated that "a minimum of specially designed Humanities courses be introduced." Currently approximately one third of the student's program is devoted to specially designated Humanities courses and seminars while the rest of the program is completed through regular departmental offerings. The first Humanities requirement is met through a sequence of courses which is designed to survey the major Humanistic achievements of Western culture from the Greco-Roman period to our own day. Each of the courses deals in different ways with its subject matter but as an example of one of the courses in the sequence, which I teach, I give the following description:

HUM 5227, Humanities. GREEK and ROMAN
The goal of this course is to provide the student with an understanding of the principal humanistic achievements of the Classical World and of the way in which those achievements have influenced, and continue to influence, Western thought. The course will begin with a discussion of the archaeological evidence for the impressive pre-Homeric origins of Greek civilization. It will then proceed to an intensive study of the achievement of Homer and of the nature of the heroic code which he celebrates in the Iliad. After a discussion of the lyric poets who bridge the gap between epic and tragedy, the course will focus on the concept of tradegy both as a significant literary genre and as a profound dimension of 5th century Athenian history. The study of tragedy will lead to an investigation of the nature of comedy as that genre was developed in the Greco-Roman world both by Aristophanes

and Plautus. Important ethical, religious, and political questions that have a lasting relevance in Western Civilization will be raised both in regard to the interaction of Socrates with the society of his time and in regard to the eloquent commentary of Lucretius that arose out of the political and social instability of the 1st century B.C. in Rome. The glorification of a transcendent political order that resolves such political and social instability, although at the price of dwarfing human individuality and freedom, will be studied, both in the achievements of the first Roman emperor, Augustus (27 B.C.-14 A.D.), and in the great epic celebration of the Augustan world view. Virgil's Aeneid. The course will then focus on the degradation of the Augustan vision which took place during the reign of terror of Nero and of the sardonic literature of anguish and rebellion which it spawned. Finally, the course, which began with the Homeric affirmation of the human capacity for heroic achievement, will reach a diametrically opposed pole as we study the satiric art of Juvenal which savagely excoriates the meanness, triviality, and ennui of much of human existence.

The analogous courses dealing with the Medieval and Renaissance period and the Modern World will utilize a different mix of literature, art, music, and philosophy but will be dedicated to a similar statement of certain principle themes which define the intellectual, spiritual, and aesthetic dimensions of the epochs with which they deal.

At the seminar level (each student must take a minimum of three seminars) the program invites scholars from all divisions of the university to develop courses that place Humanistic concerns in a larger framework or deal in an imaginative and creative way with concerns that are at the cutting edge of current humanistic thought. The program is especially hospitable to seminars that relate the concerns and methodologies of the natural sciences and the social sciences to those of the traditional Humanities. We have established an excellent relationship with the department of Physics so that each year one member of that department will teach a seminar in our program. Important contributions are regularly made to our seminar series by prominent faculty members in the departments of religion, English, Philosophy, Classics, and Dance and we anticipate that a number of other departments will be involved in the future in offering these seminars.

One of the most important seminars that has been offered in recent years in our program has been entitled "Capitalism and Human Values" and has been taught by Progressor Richard Rubenstein, Distinguished Professor of Religion. In this seminar the works of Adam Smith, Malthus, Hegel, Marx, Max Weber, Polyani, and Charles Dickens are used to illustrate the social transformation of values and the influence of social organization on human life and work.

One of the most beneficial developments that has occurred recently has been the growing association with our interdisciplinary program of members of the department of Physics. Professor Hans Plendl of that department has taught a very successful seminar entitled "The Concept of Energy from William Blake to Albert Einstein" whose scope is indicated by the following syllabus:

HUMANITIES SEMINAR 6939
The Concept of Energy from William Blake to Albert Einstein
Synopsis

In this seminar, we will discuss the relationship between the Sciences and the Humanities by focusing our attention on the concept of energy:
What is the meaning of energy in the natural sciences, in philosophy and religion, in literature and in the visual and performing arts?
What uses are made of the concept in these and other areas of human thought and action?
What are the varied forms of energy, and what are the natural laws under which they transform into one another?
How is the energy concept related to other concepts such as space/time, temperature, and entropy?
What does William Blake mean by "Energy is sheer delight" and Albert Einstein by "$E = Mc^2$"?
We will also discuss the violent outbursts of energy that marked the beginning of our universe, of our galaxy, and of the development of life on this planet, and we will consider the chances of the continuation of such life in the light of present day uses and abuses of our planetary energy resources.

Outline

Week No.		Topics:
1-4	1.	Introduction
		Sciences vs. Humanities

8

Hierarchy of the Sciences
Branches of the Physical Sciences
Macrocosm/Environment/Microcosm

Concepts of the Physical Sciences
Space/Time
2. Mass/Energy
Temperature
Entropy

The Energy Concept
Historical Origins
Forms of Energy
Conservation of Energy

3. Energy in Classical Physica/Relativity
Theory
Energy in Modern Physica/Quantum Theory

Energy and the Creation/Evolution/End
of the Universe and of Life
4. Energy and Problems of Contemporary Life

Resume-The Physical Aspects of Energy

5-8 Transition to Other Aspects of Energy

Selected Presentations by Participants
on the Energy Concept in
Literature
Performing & Visual Arts
Religion
Philosophy
Psychology
. . . .

Summary/Conclusions/Outlook

Professor Plendl has now developed a new course which
will be introduced in the current academic year which
will be entitled "The Concept of Entropy in Literature
and Science."

This year a new seminar will be introduced into
our program that will be taught by Professor John
Albright of the Physics department who is also a talented
musician and a very knowledgeable layman in the field
of theology. Professor Albright will offer a course
entitled "Chance and Causality" and he will trace the
influence of these dichotomous themes in the fields of
science, religion, and music. In the scientific area

he will be dealing with the tension between the predictable universe described by Newtonian physics and the probabilistic universe of statistical and quantum mechanics: in the area of theology he will investigate the source and nature of the opposition between the concepts of predestination and free will; and in the area of music he will examine the presuppositions behind orthodox structured musical harmonies and aleatory music. Thus, in this seminar, certain elemental forms of human thought will be examined as they express themselves in diverse subject matters.

Two recent seminars have dealt with historical orientations. In one entitled "Feudalism: Japan and Europe," Professor Charles Swain of the department of Religion examined some striking parallels in the themes of literature, art, and religious thought of medieval Japan and Western Europe. The seminar itself entered into a domain of comparative studies which on a number of issues, has only been lightly touched by existent scholarship.

In a seminar to be offered during the current academic year Professor Douglas Fowler of the department of English will investigate the interaction between the literature and social and political history in his seminar entitled "The Waste Land and Beyond." I present below the syllabus for this seminar:

Syllabus for Humanities 6939: "The Waste Land and
    Beyond"
Whatever lip-service they pay to the spirit of enquiry, in every age those people for whom ideas are more than important choose to see the order of the world in a single metaphor; for the Twentieth Century, this metaphor has been The Waste Land. T.S. Eliot's 1922 poem has exerted a force over subsequent art and thought that has been profound (and convenient) beyond all comparison; and that the contemporary world has come to be assumed as a Waste Land by the people who write poems, novels, and history--that is, by the Humanities Establishment--is a situation that one can adduce from a wide spectrum of examples and illustrations. The seminar will then attempt to (a) paraphrase and explicate the world as Eliot's poem presents it; (b) explain the durability and resonance of Eliot's construct for other imaginations; (c) examine the validity of his construct--and the rhetorical structure of that last statement is of course fair warning that it can be argued that there are alter-

native metaphors that may furnish us with other
ways of coming to terms with our world and man's
place in it.

The Waste Land is a war poem, among other
things, and it is expected that presentations for
the seminar will include discussions of the poetry
and prose of the historical moment just before the
catastrophe as well as the stories and verse created by it, and from the legacy of experience it provided for some of our most sensitive imaginations.
An essential text for one presentation will be Paul
Fussell's The Great War and Modern Memory, as well
readings from Brooke, Blunden, Sassoon, e.e. Cum-
mings, Hemingway, and historical narratives like
The Price of Glory and Gallipoli. Selections from
John Dos Passos' 1919 will be suggested for discussion.

But these readings are received ideas, and
hopefully this seminar will go beyond them. In
order to create new metaphors, we will explore
several ideas that are perhaps more subtle and un-
settling. For example, we will examine the propo-
sition that there were really not two world wars,
but a single continuing crisis from 1914 through
1945; that our historical situation is less an end-
product of the clash of ideas than of the exponen-
tial growth and importance of technology (in every
case the purest and most dangerous legacy of war);
that the great unacknowledged energies of human
nature, like jealousy or the flight from boredom or
the deathwish have been at least as important in
creating the contemporary world as the clash of
ideologies and nation-states; and that history is
really the history of the irrational. Suggested
presentations here will include (but not be limited
to) Evelyn Waugh's Brideshead Revisited, Vladimir
Nabokov's Bend Sinister, George Orwell's 1984, and
selected portions of Thomas Pynchon's Gravity Rain-
bow. We will make use of German expressionist
classics like The Cabinet of Dr. Caligari and
Metropolis, and a study of Nazi social types by
Joachim Fest called The Face of the Third Reich.

When it was initiated the Ph.D. program in the Humanities was designed to "provide a maximum of flexibility to allow almost any student to develop his special
interests, yet be a controlled and identifiable program
having most, if not all, of the traditional values of
the doctoral program." In ensuing years the program has
worked out in exactly that way. Students of varying
backgrounds but often with unique academic goals shared

with all other students in the Program the common background of the interdisciplinary courses and seminars. In recent years in any given term some forty or more students have been registered with us in some stage of the doctoral program. They are, by and large, an intellectually lively and able group and I note with genuine pleasure that even under the oppressive conditions of the current job market they have had a significant measure of success in obtaining academic positions. They have for the most part entered orthodox academic departments but have been hired also to participate in interdisciplinary work at their institutions. We feel that this illustrates the validity of our insistence on each student achieving M.A. and post M.A. competence in a subject matter field as well as mastering the interdisciplinary component that is shared by all students in the program.

For the future we plan that the program will continue to emphasize the interrelationships among the traditional humanistic disciplines and our developing understanding of the relationship between the Humanities and the natural Sciences and the Social Sciences. It will also be open to the exploration of new intellectual developments which now are only perhaps mentioned by avant garde theorists but which may later become central foundations of humanistic thought in coming decades. I can perhaps best give an indication of the range and nature of interests which the program aspires to represent and serve by indicating the current and projected themes of a series of lectures/colloquia/and performances which the interdisciplinary program in the Humanities plays a major role in sponsoring. For the current academic year the series is entitled "Rococo, Rationalism, and Revolution: The 18th Century Panorama." Next year we look forward to investigating the many significant developments that took place in the arts, politics, and the sciences in the course "Between the Wars (1918-1939)"; in 1983 in commemoration of the 500th anniversary of Martin Luther's birth, we are discussing the possibility of a program entitled "Luther: His Work, His Times, His Legacy," and in the eminently appropriate year of 1983 we are contemplating, at the suggestion of one of the physicists associated with our program, the possibility of a topic entitled "The Twenty First Century", where we can explore those developments in the arts, sciences, and humanistically oriented social sciences that are currently at the very cutting edge of their disciplines and which may give rise to new and dominant world views in the next century.

In the context of goals and aspirations of this kind, the interdisciplinary doctoral program in the Humanities at Florida State University looks forward with enthusiasm to retaining its traditional goals and modes of instruction while nurturing an interest in all that is new and valid that pertains to the Humanities. It will strive, as it has striven, to educate teachers/scholars who will make significant contributions to their profession because of a system of training, the archenemy of narrowness and pedantry, that seeks to open for them the widest possible intellectual horizons.

Leon Golden
Graduate Humanities Program

14

THE MASTER OF ARTS IN HUMANITIES
ARIZONA STATE UNIVERSITY

In Out of the Silent Planet, one of the volumes of
his space trilogy, C.S. Lewis has one of the inhabitants
of another planet remark to Ransom, the hero, that a
pleasure is not complete until it is remembered. From a
similar impulse but in a different context the great
Warburg Institute in London bears over its portal the
inscription Mnemosyne, the Greek name of the goddess of
memory, mother of the Muses. Mythically important as
the wellspring of both imagination and the recording of
the past, Mnemosyne is an appropriate name for an institution that is a specialized library and school for the
study of the survival of humanistic classical culture
in western civilization.

Cultural memory has a parallel meaning for the ASU
Humanities core faculty. For the interdisciplinary humanities faculty in the Department of Philosophy and
Humanities at Arizona State University the vitalizing
of cultural memory is at the center of their Humanities
program, both on the undergraduate and the graduate
levels. On the graduate level, especially, in the Masters of Arts in the Humanities, the interdisciplinary
departmental faculty (of five and a half tenure-track
positions) is developing a core of integrative courses
that grapple with the two pronged issue of keeping the
multifoliate study of culture alive and well in the
technologically oriented and discipline-divided context
of the modern University. The prongs of the issue include, of course, the responsibility of all serious
scholars to the body of advanced disciplinary knowledge
and the equally strong obligation to the complexly integrated structures of history and culture.

The relation between the core courses and the
selected body of disciplinary courses in the Master of
Arts in the Humanities program support from another
direction the necessary balance between disciplinary
depth and sound integrative exploration. On an administrative level the relation between the small core of
interdisciplinary faculty in the Department of Philosophy and Humanities and the Committee on Humanities, a
group of ten Humanities faculty serving as a trans-
college policy committee (under the Graduate College)
for the M.A. degree, also reflects the vital link between the two fundamental obligations for sound and
innovative interdisciplinary study: disciplinary depth
and imaginative breadth.

General Description

The Master of Arts in Humanities is an individualized interdisciplinary degree that integrates graduate courses in two or more departments to provide an academic foundation for research leading to a thesis in the humanities. Although it has been recently restructured, some form of it has existed for about fifteen years at Arizona State. Topics for theses require a general understanding of cultural history or of particular times in history when the relationships between cultural values and one or more of the arts have illuminated the important human questions. Generally speaking, theses have in the past been focused upon relationships between the usual humanities disciplines, but the intention of the Committee is not to exclude humanistic approaches to topics that might be based in the sciences or engineering. Faculty in the program are particularly interested in studies that deal with interpretations of culture.

The Committee on Humanities is the over-arching administrative committee under the Graduate College. The Committee itself is trans-college and interdisciplinary; it functions in setting policy and supervising programs of study leading to the Master of Arts degree in Humanities. The present committee is composed of members from the following departments: Art, Dance, English, Foreign Languages, History, Music, Philosophy and Humanities, Religious Studies, and Theatre. Courses and concentrations are not limited, however, to those faculty and departments. It is understood that the sciences, social sciences, education, and engineering may also be approached from a humanistic perspective.

All students must apply to the program through the Graduate College. In addition to Graduate requirements, students must submit GRE scores and three letters of academic recommendation to the Chairperson of the Committee on the Master of Arts in the Humanities. Students whose applications are completed by March 1 will be advised of their admission status by April 1. Qualified students applying after March 1 may be admitted if openings are available. Students who fulfill general requirements of the Graduate College and have B.A. degrees in any one of the humanities disciplines listed by the National Endowment for the Humanities are usually welcomed into the program: English or comparative literature, ancient or modern languages, art history, philosophy, religious studies, history, music or cultural anthropology. In addition to (or as part of) this degree, it is desirable that students have a strong general education, with at least introductory courses in two of the following: history, literature, art, religion, theatre, music, philosophy, and civilization.

An individual program of study, including courses in interdisciplinary humanities and related disciplines in the College of Fine Arts or Liberal Arts, is selected in consultation with the student's supervisory committee in order to form a coherent graduate program. Ordinarily the program will consist of 36 hours credit (including 6 hours of thesis) and will include at least a core of 9 hours of 500-level interdisciplinary courses offered within the Department of Philosophy and Humanities. Areas of concentration will include a maximum of 21 hours of course work usually to be distributed in two or more of the disciplinary departments. The program is designed to be flexible enough to allow a student to emphasize areas of study within the humanities.

Requirements for the interdisciplinary humanities degree (36 hours) include:

A. Thesis HUP 599 (6 hours) (Prefix may be from other Humanities disciplines)

B. Integrative humanities course (9-12 hours)

    HUP 501 Cultural Synthesis
    HUP 502 Esthetics
    HUP 591 Seminars in Topics (that focus interdisciplinary research and interests).
    Some topics include:

    a. Pre-Raphaelites
    b. Iconography of Death: 1590-1620
    c. Topics in Myth
    d. Post-Impressionism and Culture
    e. East-West Esthetics
    f. English Culture and the European Renaissance

C. Courses in a disciplinary concentration, relating two disciplines or representing area studies. (18-21 hours)

The following are examples of three possible patterns of concentration, although these patterns are not intended to be exclusive.

1) Courses in the English Department focusing a genre interest in lyric poetry. (18 hours)

ENG 545 Studies in English Literature
ENG 442 20th Century British Poetry
ENG 427 The Age of Johnson
ENG 425 Romantic Poetry
ENG 419 The Age of Donne
ENG 520 Renaissance Literature

2)   A. Courses in art history and literature that focus the theory of satire and comedy. (18 hours distributed by advisement)

or

B. Courses in philosophy and literature that focus the theory of satire and comedy. (18 hours distributed by advisement)

3)   Renaissance Studies

ENG 421 Shakespeare
ENG 520 Renaissance Literature
SPA 434 The Golden Age
HIS 590 Renaissance/Reformation
ARH 434 Renaissance Art
MHL 536 Music of the Renaissance

4)   Religion and Science

ENG 591   Darwinism
PHI 591   Social and Moral Philosophy
REL 541-42 Issues in Contemporary Theology
PHY 464   Elements of Nuclear Physics
HIS 512   European Historiography

Relevant History

Arizona State University, in the Phoenix suburb of Tempe, is a former teachers' college which has rapidly turned into an urban university in the last fifteen years or so. Its origins contributed a lasting emphasis on the value of teaching, an emphasis both admirable and unusual for an institution of its size and present research accomplishment. The enrollment is about 30,000 and respectable doctoral programs exist in most of the major disciplines. Adequate financial support comes from the state of Arizona, which allocates a budget similar to that given the University of Arizona in Tucson, with its nearly equal student population. Unlike the University of Arizona, however, its students are drawn almost entirely from the local residents of Phoenix, and at least half of them commute. A high percentage of its students also hold full or part-time jobs; their attitude toward their education is correspondingly in the direction of improving their economic position. The vision of the student body is focused upon upward social mobility, with little exception. The student body is national in origin in the sense that most of their families have moved to Phoenix in the last five to ten years.

The curriculum is comparable to that at a Big Ten university. A large proportion of the faculty (who total 1300 in ranks) have degrees from the Big Ten, just as most of the residents of Phoenix have recently moved from the Midwest.

The nearby city of Phoenix is prosperous and endowed with cultural resources, and our university library is a moderately good research center which also provides good undergraduate services.

The program in which the current interdisciplinary M.A. had its origin was that of the Humanities and Religious Studies Department in the College of Fine Arts, formerly a Center for the Humanities, approximately twenty years old. The Department attached to itself a small but strong program of religious studies, which was created and nourished over the past few years by the Humanities faculty.

Within the past twenty-odd years of its existence the program had grown from one or two team-taught courses administered by one resident faculty member to a fully developed major, consisting of a core of integrated interdisciplinary courses and two areas of disciplinary depth in associated humanities departments (mostly literature, art, music, philosophy) with a full-time resident faculty of nine, hired mainly from the disciplines of literature, art history, music, and humanities education.

The program also included a Master of Arts degree, usually a two-year program of interdisciplinary course work with a disciplinary and period focus, both culminating in a master's thesis. In addition to a resident faculty, the Department had approximately eight adjunct part-time faculty to field off-campus residence credit courses.

When the former chairman of the Department applied for the NEH Consultancy Grant in the Summer of 1978, the Department of Humanities and Religious Studies at Arizona State University was trying to resolve problems

associated with offering an arts and ideas curriculum
leading towards the B.A. and M.A. in Humanities with an
arts and education faculty. The Religious Studies
faculty, which had for a number of years offered the
history of ideas within the program, was at the point
of establishing a separate department and curriculum.
The remaining nine Humanities faculty within the Department were Ph.D.'s from various disciplines within the
humanities and from humanities education, with the exception of one M.A. in Humanities (from our own program)
who was in the process of getting a Ph.D. in Humanities
Education. The approach to humanities curriculum of
each group was related to its graduate education: (1)
the faculty with Ph.D.'s in traditional humanities disciplines were (with one exception) committed to courses
that approached the interdisciplinary questions from a
strong disciplinary base; and (2) the faculty with
humanities education backgrounds were devoted to a
transdisciplinary approach. In more concrete terms,
the faculty with the stronger disciplinary perspective
favored interdisciplinary courses based in traditional
research and analysis, while those with humanities education backgrounds and interests often favored courses
with popular topics that relied heavily upon media presentation and the experience of the humanities. Both
groups, however, were committed to team teaching on the
general studies level.

At this stage in the development of the program the
chair was seeking from the consultancy a way of moder-
ating the philosophic split within the department and
constructing a coherent curriculum that would make the
best of the strengths of both faculty groups. One of
the major problems was size; the faculty was not large
enough for each group to go its own way. It badly
needed the help of history-of-ideas faculty in the University. The reputation of the program was low in the
eyes of some in the University-at-large because people
were teaching subjects for which they did not have credentials. This lack of specialized expertise was especially a problem for the graduate program and upper
level courses in general.

The four major questions asked in the summary of
the NEH grant proposal were these: (1) What are possible
modes for greater interdisciplinary out-reach in the
University? (2) By what means could faculty limit some
of the department projects in order to focus energies
and abilities? (3) Where should major energies go? (4)
How best can the Department develop the highest quality
program in the study of ideas and values? In the back-

20

ground, even at this stage, was always the question of whether the Department should request transfer to the Liberal Arts College from its present place in Fine Arts.

The selection of Dr. Charles Muscatine of the University of California at Berkeley as NEH consultant turned out to be enormously helpful in answering these questions and restructuring the humanities curriculum in a fruitful way. Dr. Muscatine's first visit and report in the Fall 1978 pinpointed several major problems in the curriculum: (1) the tendency to present materials to students in the introductory team courses in overly smooth packages, which exposed only the superficially parallel relationships between styles in the arts and a few ideas of the culture; (2) the corollary lack of stimulus to involvement of the student in exploring vital intellectual issues which could not be seen as "fitting" the interdisciplinary package; (3) the teaching of advanced humanities courses outside the faculty person's expertise, especially a problem on the graduate level; (4) the organization of courses into broad surveys that needed to be more realistically limited in focus, both for the sake of faculty expertise and student ability to command the material; (5) the need for at least one general studies course that explored vital contemporary issues in a way to display the intellectual strengths of the program for further study; (6) the lack of coherence in the graduate program. As a result of these problems Dr. Muscatine very tactfully suggested several possibilities to the faculty: (1) some changes in course structure, towards opening issues rather than closing them; (2) developing a Contemporary Issues "show-case" course; (3) a greater "brokering" of the graduate program. For the graduate program, such advice would result in encouraging students to take advantage of the courses and expertise already available in the University and in developing fewer courses on the graduate level, especially ones that were close to faculty research interests.

Faculty responded well to the suggestions, although naturally there was some concern over Dr. Muscatine's interpretation of University attitudes towards the program as it existed. Some faculty were made uneasy by indications that the Humanities program was not in line with the future plans and direction of the College of Fine Arts, and some of the faculty were concerned about the University's intensified thrust towards research which in some sense threatened the position of the program and the emphasis on teaching at the heart of its tradition.

Fortunately, the tension caused by not knowing the future was allayed later in the spring semester by indications of the new structuring. In fact, by Dr. Muscatine's February visit, there were administrative indications that the major part of the program with attendant degrees would be transferred to Liberal Arts. Curriculum plans during his second visit were adjusted to that possible future, though it was not clear at that time whether the program would be under a single Humanities Department or Center for Interdisciplinary Studies, or whether the Humanities faculty would provide part of a dual-structured department.

During the Spring of 1979 the Provost decided to create a joint Department of Philosophy and Humanities with the understanding that Philosophy faculty should participate to a limited extent in the Humanities program so as to provide some of the history-of-ideas component and so that the Humanities program might in turn provide Philosophy with a broader community outreach. In more general terms, the merger provided a structure for an unusual department with many possibilities for serving the humanistic needs of the University. The division of the faculty (with the education-oriented groups transferred to the Secondary Education Department) changed somewhat the objectives of the original grant proposal, as there was no longer a need to reconcile the two philosophies of interdisciplinary humanities. At the same time, humanities faculty moving to the new Philosophy/Humanities Department and the College of Liberal Arts needed more consultancy time for adaptation. Similarly, humanities education faculty could benefit from suggestions appropriate to their new direction.

Major concerns emerging from the restructuring were these: (1) How could the Humanities faculty in Philosophy and Humanities, now reduced to five, exclusive of several part-time Adjunct faculty and six half-time teaching assistants offer both a B.A. and an M.A. in Humanities? (2) What shape should the Contemporary Issues course take in the new structure? Would it not be wise to postpone its organization? (3) How could the Humanities curriculum benefit from the new accessibility of Philosophy faculty without being overwhelmed by the ideas approach? (4) How could Humanities faculty from within a Joint department cultivate fruitful interdisciplinary relationships with faculty from other disciplines in both Liberal Arts and Fine Arts?

Dr. Muscatine helped the Humanities faculty both

to focus these concerns as central and also at least to
begin to think through their resolution. Obviously, they
are ongoing concerns, but both philosophy faculty and humanities interdisciplinary faculty under a philosophy chair
who understands the goals of both programs now have what
they feel to be creative directions for their solution.

(1) To begin with, relationships between faculties
are growing and deepening in mutual support. There is
a real sense in which there is a dual department with
some unified vision of service to the University on the
General Studies level. At the same time Humanities
faculty has major control over its curriculum. Though
they have not yet developed a joint Contemporary Issues
course, they have developed less formal intellectual
relationships (exchange of lectures and other exchanges)
that will bear fruit later. They shall be hiring a new
line this year to develop the Contemporary Issues course.
At the same time faculties have come to appreciate differences in approach in a way that will help them to
make use of the strengths of both. At present, three
members of the Philosophy faculty are teaching in our
courses, and plans for the cultural history sequence at
the heart of our major will include participation by
both a classical philosopher and a Kantian. The philos-
opher-chairman of the Department has been particularly
supportive of the Humanities curriculum and offered
lectures last year in both introductory courses. The
Department also has recently established a Center for
Ethics that can be a meeting ground for both faculties.
By efficient planning and rotation, Humanities faculty
can still offer the major in humanities.

(2) Inevitably, the shape of the Humanities program has shifted somewhat from Fine Arts to Liberal
Arts and ideas, but, with the help of Dr. Muscatine,
faculty have prepared new catalogue copy that maintains
some of the old important links with art history, dance,
and aesthetics. The new curriculum has now been approved
at both the Department and the College levels.

(3) The most radical shift within the curriculum
is the restructuring of the M.A. program since the
Winter of 1980 offered by a cross-college Committee on
the Humanities, composed of representatives from ten
departments. Student programs are being individually
tailored and yet monitored for coherence by the Committee. At the same time the core Humanities faculty in
the Department of Philosophy and Humanities is developing several seminars that focus upon integrative interdisciplinary methodology. These courses are designed

to become the particular field or territory of the core group, which will continue to do initial advisement and "housekeeping" for the Master of Arts. Although the venture is comparatively new, both core faculty and interdisciplinary faculty are immensely pleased with the new structure.

During 1980-81 at the advice of Dr. Muscatine the Humanities core faculty concentrated upon a course called Cultural Synthesis, which is cross-listed as a seminar in ten Humanities departments throughout the University. The Dean of the Graduate School offered financial support for the course so that six prominent scholars in the problems of interpreting culture could be brought in for lectures and seminar presentations. Those who came last year in the Fall are Carl E. Schorske, Princeton, author of Fin de Siècle Vienna; Svetlana Alpers, Berkeley, who finished a book the year before at the Institute of Advanced Study; and Stephen Greenblatt, Berkeley, productive scholar in Renaissance literature and culture. Those scholars scheduled for Spring of '81 were Stephen G. Nichols, comparative literature, Dartmouth; Barney Childs, music, Redlands; and Jonathan Z. Smith, history of religions, The University of Chicago. For 1981-82 Charles Muscatine, Timothy J. Clark, Homer Swander, Lord Asa Briggs, and Peter Gay are scheduled to lecture. Both faculty and students read and prepare for the outside lectures, and the Humanities core faculty has been greatly stimulated.

Humanities faculty are currently in the process of establishing a firm interdisciplinary territory within the University. Recent hirings, a historian of science and a nineteenth-century cultural historian from Yale, illustrate a movement towards a stronger, more balanced Humanities curriculum, firmly based in sound research. The addition of the young woman in History of Science creates important possibilities for the bridging of the "two cultures."

Towards the Interpretation of Culture:
A Core of Graduate Interdisciplinary Courses
in the Humanities

The three interdisciplinary courses to serve as core for the newly structured Master of Arts in Humanities under the Graduate College are a natural outgrowth of the curriculum study undertaken during the past two years by the Humanities faculty in the Department of Philosophy and Humanities at Arizona State University. Such a program defines a place for the interdisciplinary

Humanities faculty and answers a fundamental intellectual need within the discrete and fragmented Humanities disciplines that represent the prevailing structure of Humanities departments in research Universities today. The Humanities faculty plans to offer during 1981-82 a group of three courses: Cultural Synthesis (6 hours); Aesthetics: Theory of Art (3 hours); and Renaissance: Narratives of Becoming (3 hours).

The three new courses represent the 12-hour core of the newly structured Master of Arts in Humanities. Cultural Synthesis is a 6-hour, two-semester course; Aesthetics: Theory of Art, a 3-hour, one-semester course; and Renaissance: Narratives of Becoming, a 3-hour, one-semester course. All three are interdisciplinary Humanities courses, intended to offer the interdisciplinary graduate student methodology and practice in integrating various aspects of culture. Students enrolling in the new Master of Arts program have the opportunity of constructing under the direction of their Supervisory Committee an individualized program of interdisciplinary study. Although they will be required to take 9-12 hours of the core, they will structure their remaining 18-21 hours around the courses representing their strengths and interests, always with the guiding principle that their program should be designed to culminate in a sound research thesis (6 hours).

Cultural Synthesis

Because of the lack of funds and release time for planning, Cultural Synthesis is being run for the second time this year under the coordination of Dr. Doebler, a literary scholar in the English Renaissance, Dr. Kotrozo, an art historian and aesthetician, and Dr. Charles Dellheim, as a workshop. All Humanities faculty are attending, and discussions between faculty and students are exposing problems and often hidden assumptions in the "doing" of cultural history, particularly in using the arts and particular artifacts as foci through which the student can examine other values of the culture. The five faculty participating feel that they have not been able to develop the conceptual structure fully for the course, mainly because of lack of release time for planning and reading. Faculty are requesting grant monies to ease that problem. It becomes increasingly obvious that the next step is to develop a more selective intellectual framework that focuses the issues of particular importance to the kind of cultural history and arts and ideas program offered by the Department.

The newly structured course itself will focus for next year on selected publication and theory of the lecturers coming this year and that of the lecturers coming next year. Readings for last year included Carl E. Schorske's Fin De Siècle Vienna; Stephen Greenblatt's Sir Walter Raleigh; Clifford Geertz's Interpretations of Culture, and various essays from current journals. Even during the preliminary run-through Humanities faculty became sensitized to the major issues around which they plan to organize the course: style and content; taste; issues surrounding the identification of root metaphors; problems of relating socio-economic structures to artistic values; continuity in the development of the arts; synchronicity of the arts; theories of culture. Particularly interesting are practical ways to resolve the tension between the temporal and the transcendent in human culture.

One of the distinguished lecturers commented on the program after his visit in the following way:

This was my first visit to ASU (and for that matter, to the state of Arizona), and I was grateful for the warm and hospitable reception. But above all-- and this is the purpose of my letter--I was impressed with the intelligence and innovative design of the new Humanities Program with its required course in "Cultural Synthesis." The conception of this course displays a sensitivity to what is unquestionably among the most exciting developments in the Humanities and Social Sciences at this time, namely, an interest in shared structures and meanings that can only be interpreted by crossing traditional disciplinary boundaries. The program's design is equally impressive and effective. It is one thing to have outside lecturers--virtually all colleges and universities of any distinction have a more or less steady stream of them. It is quite another thing to have lecturers contribute directly to an on-going intellectual and pedagogical project. Here the colloquium seminar conception is crucial: the combination of the formal lecture and the seminar on the following day prevents what so often happens, even with the best intentions in the world, namely, a highly formal and demanding lecture followed by a little party where social decorum keeps the conversation entirely free from intellectual exchange or, alternately, a low-key visit without a public lecture to crystallize the central issues.

Aesthetics: Theory of Art*

The aesthetics course is to be taught by the Departmental art-historian aesthetician (Ph.D. from the University of California at Los Angeles) and represents a culmination of her nine-year's development in the field of aesthetics, a rare specialty for art historians. Increasingly, the faculty has seen her modes of evaluation as central to our program, but it hopes especially in terms of the newly structured graduate course to work out a stronger interdisciplinary structure.

The course will be a mixture of lecture and seminar discussion with lectures predominantly by Dr. Kotrozo and guest lectures by other team members. If time is available, other faculty members will sit in and participate in discussion, in order to build the sense of mutually understood interdisciplinary framework among the Humanities interdisciplinary faculty.

Although aesthetics is traditionally a branch of philosophy and can be presented as an examination of the logical consistency, coherency, and plausibility of propositions concerning works of art, it can also be taught from a humanistic perspective. This course investigates many of the conventional issues in aesthetics as they can be applied to music, art history, dance, and theatre with a focus on common problems faced by the critics and practioners in these fields.

The first unit of the course introduces and defines aesthetics and proceeds to discuss the value of philosophic exploration in the arts in the contemporary world. This is followed by historical readings which illustrate the origin of many of the presuppositions about art we hold in the present. For example, Immanuel Kant is associated with the controversial "aesthetic attitude theory" which divorces the work of art from practical ends and sets it apart from life in an autonomous contemplative realm of pure experience (of beauty). Recent theorists discuss, criticize, and update his views. Edward Bullough's classic article "Psychic Distance," and John Dewey's "Having an Experience" head the list of contemporary selections.

Other units in the course tackle such issues as the relationship of art and science in the search for

_____

*I am indebted to Dr. Carol Kotrozo for the description of the aesthetics course.

truth, the issue of art and morality and the role of the aesthetician in arbitrating disputes in the area of obscenity, the problem of defining art and the role of language toward this end (essential versus operational definitions, Wittgenstein's theory of language), and the meaning of common terms of categories in art criticism (such as realism, naturalism, abstraction, classicism, stylization, etc.)

A major portion of the course is devoted to some of the basic theories of art as criteria of evaluation. For example, the imitation theory (mimesis in literature) is discussed, comparing its application to literature and the visual arts. Plato, Aristotle, and Reynolds as historical proponents are contrasted with contemporary views of E.H. Gombrich and Abrams (The Mirror and the Lamp). The expression theory follows, correlated with nineteenth-century romanticism and its counterpart in the twentieth century (German Expressionism and Abstract Expressionism). Theories of Tolstoy, Collingwood, Ducasse, and Reig are among the best in the area. The Intentional Fallacy, as an offshoot of the expression theory, is an interesting and significant side issue.

Psychological theories based on Freud and Jung are included in the course material as well as the modern formalist theories. Again, these theories are applied to various art forms (Hamlet and Leonardo receive a large portion of the attention in this unit).

The student is encouraged to explore, analyze, and evaluate these materials and to arrive at a personal philosophy of the arts which will form the basis of aesthetic contemplation and intellectual judgment. The student keeps a detailed journal which includes essay answers to such questions as: "Some say that only science gives us truth; fine art can only create a make-believe world which may be psychologically entertaining, playful, sensational, or therapeutic, but in any case has a function which is trivial compared to that of science. Is this true, or can fine art create ideas and icons signifying a real world which is or may be?"

Renaissance: Narratives of Becoming

This new one-semester course embodies the interdisciplinary approach to reality (and history) both in its organization and its approach to the materials.

28

Taught by a literary critic and historian with a specialty in the Renaissance, the course focuses on literary artifacts of the period, particularly those with central narrative metaphors, e.g., The Faerie Queene and Paradise Lost. Less directly illustrative but still with internal narrative patterns of action, a history play and a tragedy by Shakespeare are included among the reading assignments. Lyric poetry will be assigned as celebrations of moments within an implied narrative of pilgrimage.

Narrative patterns will be related to the root metaphor of the Judaeo-Christian-classical synthesis that characterizes the style and major assumptions of the English verbal Renaissance. Necessarily, cultural artifacts, verbal and visual, artistic and historical, will be explored as well as literature. Appropriate critical and scholarly reading will be assigned, among the secondary materials Kermode's Genesis of Secrecy; Hayden White's Metahistory; Greenblatt's Sir Walter Raleigh; Chastel's Age of Humanism; Levin's Myth of the Golden Age; Tuve's Elizabethan and Metaphysical Imagery; Colie's Paradoxica Epidemica; Panofsky's Studies in Iconology, and others. Particular attention will be given to major symbols of the period, which are both integrally (and sometimes by implication) related to the structural narratives against which Elizabethans and Jacobeans integrated their values. Particularly important are the figure of death, that of the Neoplatonic Venus, the symbol of the crown, and the courtier as politician and lover.

This course will usually be run in the Spring semester. The major strategy of organization is a combination of lecture and discussion. Essay tests with some recognition of important literary quotations will be scheduled for mid-term and final in addition to a research paper that focuses relationships between some aspect of narrative in a literary work and other elements of the culture surrounding it. Particular attention will be directed to constructing the topics towards issues that reflect change or continuity in the culture.

Participants in the three courses

All five (or more) Humanities faculty will participate in the Cultural Synthesis. Four of the faculty have taught interdisciplinary courses for the past four to ten years. In the Fall Dr. Doebler (Renaissance literary historian) and Dr. Dellheim (cultural historian) will plan and coordinate the course with the other three giving guest lectures and consistently participating in the discussion. In the Spring Dr. Kotrozo (art historian-aesthetician) and Dr. Doebler will coordinate the semester, while the other three faculty will guest lecture and participate in the discussions. The course will meet formally for 2-3 hours each week, while the faculty will meet for a planning session two hours each week.

The Aesthetics: Theory of Art course and the Renaissance: Narratives of Becoming will meet once weekly, with the Aesthetics: Theory of Art course running in the Fall and the Renaissance: Narratives of Becoming in the Spring. Dr. Kotrozo (art historian) will teach the aesthetics course with guest participations, while Dr. Doebler will be primarily responsible for Renaissance: Narratives of Becoming.

The students in all three courses are likely to be beginning graduate students in the interdisciplinary Humanities M.A. program. At the same time, in the Cultural Synthesis course particularly, we are hoping to involve disciplinary Humanities faculty, particularly those serving from both Fine and Liberal Arts on the Committee on Humanities. One of the interesting possibilities for this course is that it is on the way to becoming a colloquium meeting ground for scholars throughout the University who share an interest in culture.

The administration at Arizona State University, particularly the Graduate College, is committed to continuing the interdisciplinary M.A. in Humanities and has shown strong support of the core program. Strong evidence of this commitment is the yearly funding for the lecture series to stimulate research.

Evaluation

Our evaluation plan for the program includes two two-day visits by an outside consultant who will evaluate the quality of the courses and the degree to which they fulfill the objectives of the core: (1) to develop an interdisciplinary methodology based on an awareness of crucial problems in interpreting culture; (2) to explore theories or strategies by which to handle such problems creatively; (3) within the proposed graduate structure to develop an "integrative" historical imagination.

It is too soon to say how well the new structuring

30

of the core courses and of the new administration is working. There is currently great enthusiasm among those who value interdisciplinary studies. From the Chairs of the disciplinary departments there is a more measured support. There is, however, a general agreement that the new structure is budgetarily efficient and at the same time has good possibilities for academic quality. The potentiality is there for core courses that take advantage of the particular expertise of the Humanities interdisciplinary faculty. At the same time the new broader administrative structure of the Committee on Humanities provides a channel for communication and the location of scholarly expertise within the University.

The program is, of course, designed not for the ordinary student and not for the student who wants a smattering of this and that, but for the unusual student whose interests in the realities of culture strain against disciplinary boundaries and demand the possibility of exploration.

Bettie Anne Doebler
Department of Philosophy
and Humanities

32

INTERDISCIPLINARY EDUCATION
AT AN UPPER-DIVISION COLLEGE
THE PENNSYLVANIA STATE UNIVERSITY

The Capitol Campus of Penn State has experimented with a number of innovative and interdisciplinary programs during the last fifteen years. While some of the experiments have failed, others have proved successful enough to have been adopted as permanent parts of the curriculum. This report includes a description of some of the successful programs, a brief history of the campus as a context for that description, a discussion of the identity problems faced by an upper-division and graduate center as well as an examination of the problems encountered in implementing general education goals at this campus. Capitol is a unique part of the Penn State system and many of its problems are local ones related to the campus mission in the Central Pennsylvania area. But other problems, such as the integration of general education into professional training programs or the role of the Humanities at an upper-division campus, are common to many other types of institutions. The lessons learned at Capitol may help other colleges evaluate their own interdisciplinary programs and, perhaps, contribute directly to the current debate on the survival of humanistic or liberal education in this technological age.

This report reflects my personal views on the history and development of the campus, gained from interviews with the original faculty whenever possible and on conversations with current faculty and staff whose assistance I gratefully wish to acknowledge. Capitol Campus is currently reconsidering and redesigning its undergraduate and graduate programs in preparation for a change from a term to a semester calendar in 1983. The comments presented in this essay, therefore, reflect on the accomplishments of the last fifteen years and suggest what I take to be modest plans for the future.

The Campus: Relationships Between its Mission and General Education

The Capitol Campus of Penn State was established in 1966, as the first upper-division and graduate center in Pennsylvania.[1] It is the only institution of its type in the State and the only one of the twenty university campuses given the specific mission of developing innovative and interdisciplinary programs at the undergraduate and graduate levels. Although such a mission statement may rekindle memories of the academic reforms of the late 1960s, Capitol's birth was not the result of a desire to create an alternative to the traditional system of higher education in Pennsylvania. The Governor of the State and the President of the University conceived the idea of locating a Penn State campus in Middletown as a means of lessening the economic impact of a Department of Defense decision to close the Olmsted Air Force Base. Although the Governor was concerned with saving jobs and utilizing the soon to be abandoned buildings, Dr. Eric Walker, Penn State's President, saw a greater benefit for the University. He believed that, "an upper-division and graduate institution...would complement the efforts of neighboring institutions and relieve some of the enrollment strain on the University Park campus."[2] Thus an unusual set of circumstances led to the development of a unique campus with a mission different from that of the other University campuses.

Capitol's mission was unusual because its academic programs were to address the need for post-baccalaureate education in Central Pennsylvania and to offer a higher level of professional education for the area's many employed residents. Given that context, being "innovative" meant that : (1) new academic programs such as engineering technology and psychosocial science would be developed, (2) community needs in social services and public administration would play a large role in the design of specific curricula, (3) the academic programs would be grouped by general subject areas rather than organized into traditional departments, and (4) teaching techniques would emphasize student-centered learning and independent study programs because of the student body's diverse personal and educational backgrounds.[3]

The second part of the campus mission--the pursuit of interdisciplinary studies--was more difficult to implement because the purposes, methods, and benefits of interdisciplinary education were not clear. There were few successful models that could be adapted to this particular type of institution and many of the models that did exist were flawed.[4] While the reasons for developing interdisciplinary programs were partly the result of a desire to avoid duplicating programs at neighboring colleges, there was also a real challenge in trying to accomplish something new at this campus. The potential benefits of interdisciplinary studies promised students a more enriching educational experience. As Vincent Kavaloski observed:

34

While specific conceptions of interdisciplinarity and hence of interdisciplinary education vary considerably, the arguments advanced in favor of virtually all these forms appear to share a common conceptual structure, insofar as they draw upon a common body of desiderata:

(1) Integration of knowledge. Interdisciplinary education aims at being an intrinsically integrative learning experience for the student, i.e., it encourages the student to perceive the various components of human knowledge within some larger holistic framework.

(2) Freedom of inquiry. Interdisciplinary education stimulates a greater freedom of inquiry than conventional disciplinary education.

(3) Innovation. Interdisciplinary education is thought to have a greater chance of getting students to break out of narrow, conventional lines of thinking and to attain something akin to original insights.[5]

The first group of faculty subscribed to these principles, as demonstrated in their design of two general core courses for the students at Capitol. The two courses were entitled "Argumentation, Rhetoric," and "Human Behavior and Man, Culture, and Technology." The original plan gave a team of teachers from different disciplines the task of demonstrating how the methods of inquiry and criticism could be applied to the study of contemporary problems, such as the impact of technology on the individual and society. Although the courses were interdisciplinary in the sense that several scholars would approach a problem by means of the methodology and subject matter of their own disciplines, the real purpose of the two courses was to broaden the relevance of general education courses. By compressing general education goals into two courses and teaching those courses in an innovative manner, the course planners hoped to create a sense of collegiality and to introduce students to a broader understanding of human values in modern society. That viewpoint implied a specific understanding of the kind of educational experience students at Capitol should share and is similar to the one recommended by Daniel Bell in his report on the reforms contemplated by Columbia in the mid-sixties. Bell argued that:

For the younger student, it is important that the college experience be unhampered and distinctive. It should be the testing years--the testing of one's self and one's values; the exploration of

35

different fields before settling in to a single one; and the experience of belonging to a common intellectual community in which diverse fields of knowledge are commingled. In short, college can still be one of the few places of broad intellectual adventure, the place where one can resist, momentarily, the harness that society now seeks to impose at an earlier and earlier stage on its youth.[6]

Capitol's founding faculty shared that call to adventure, that image of a new campus dedicated to the design of a different kind of education. But they realized that Bell's ideal intellectual community could not be built at a two-year institution where the average age of the students was twenty-seven. Bell's proposal for the addition of a third tier to the college curriculum was more in keeping with the mission of an upper-division campus. His definition of the third tier is remarkably similar to the descriptions of some of Capitol's early programs. In Bell's words:

The third tier is a synoptic program, at the senior level, whose purpose is two-fold: to deal with the methodological and philosophical (and in the case of the social sciences, historical) presuppositions of a field; to show the application of the discipline to general problems, or to issues requiring a multidisciplinary approach, in order to see the operation of the discipline in a wider context.[7]

This program could be justified on the grounds that general education could be an important institution goal if a college was willing to design courses "which cut across disciplinary lines...to deal with the history, tradition and great works of Western civilization and courses which deal with the integrative problems or common subject matters of several disciplines."[8]

While nothing in any of Bell's proposals ran contrary to the goals of Capitol's first academic programs, no two courses could ever accomplish what Bell had in mind. The general core courses were a compromise that took into consideration the desire to be innovative or interdisciplinary and measured that desire against the fact that Capitol's general education goals had to be integrated into preprofessional training programs. While Bell's ideas had little influence on the way Capitol's academic programs were organized, his views of the reforms contemplated at Columbia do reflect what many of the early faculty thought about the mission of this campus. There is no question that the faculty wanted our students to be more highly-trained technologists or skilled business managers. They hoped that Capitol's graduates would have a broader view of life and learning. That is why the general core courses were considered important during the years when curricular experiments occupied the attention of the faculty.

The true test of the goals and contents of both core courses came when they were tried in the classroom, a test that both of them failed. As far as I can determine, the courses were offered only three times between 1967 and 1971. Even though they were never scheduled after 1971, both courses can still be found in the current (1981-82) catalog. Their failure was due in part to the course designer's tenuous assumptions about the advanced student's interest in such courses and on other factors which interfered with the implementation of a required core for all students at this campus.

The first factor was a dramatic increase in enrollment, an increase which demonstrated that Business Administration and Engineering Technology were likely to be the most successful programs on campus. The student body increased from 18 in 1966 to 1,647 in 1969; the number of faculty climbed from 8 to 72. Not all of the new staff shared the general education views of the original group and most of them were selected because of their expertise in specialized areas. A second factor was that, even though the pool of faculty available to teach the core courses had grown, the number interested in doing so did not. The content of the courses also proved to be an important problem; but the greatest difficulty, besides the compatibility of the individuals involved in the mandatory team-teaching approach, was in the selection of teachers who could "develop the capacity to meet various fields of knowledge on their own terms, especially by understanding and respecting the epistemologies and methodologies which underlie those fields with which they will work, and to build a vocabulary that can be precisely understood across the fields of knowledge."[9]

Finally, even enthusiastic faculty members realized that they could not spend a disproportionate amount of time planning the core courses, while simultaneously trying to complete the design of an entire curriculum. Because the educational philosophy of the institution was still being formulated, it was not altogether clear how the general core could become an integral part of

37

that philosophy.

Few of the faculty noticed, and fewer still were disappointed with, the failure of the core courses, especially since so many more prestigious institutions had failed to implement the idea of a common intellectual experience for their students. Although the Harvard example is probably the best known, many educators throughout the country had begun to doubt the usefulness of core courses. Critics charged that: "There is simply too much knowledge for any one set of courses to survey it even in a superficial way, and there is not a consensus among reasonable men as to what knowledge is most fundamental or what that educated man should know."[10] Such skepticism is reflected in the trend toward specialization that dominated higher education during the period of Capitol's infancy. Frederick Rudolph's "survey of curricular developments and course selections between 1967 and 1974 confirmed persistent trends--increased specialization, choice of electives in the field of concentration, the increase of electives at the expense of general education but not at the expense of majors."[11] Gerald Grant noted that a study of student transcripts during the same period revealed that: "Students used their increased elective power not to substitute other broad-gauged requirements in the liberal arts but to concentrate more heavily in one area."[12]

While Capitol had created several innovative and interdisciplinary programs in the Humanities and Social Sciences by 1976, a catalog survey released by the Carnegie Commission during that year revealed that student interest in interdisciplinary studies was small. Interdisciplinary majors were found at 53 percent of the 270 colleges surveyed, but only 6.4 percent of the students chose them.[13] Capitol's enrollments indicated that interdisciplinary programs could attract new students even though the enrollments were likely to remain small. But the future of the campus could not depend on the strength of a few small programs. It had to be based on finding ways to integrate some of the courses offered in those programs with the general educational philosophy of the institution. The general core courses had not accomplished that and there is little evidence that the faculty as a whole ever believed that they would.

The largest programs on the campus were concerned with vocational training. The Business Administration and Engineering Technology programs adopted a minimum distribution requirement rather than questioning how such a requirement might fit into the general educational goals of the campus. If Capitol's faculty had been genuinely committed to a limited general education program, the decision which allowed an Engineering Technology major to take any two courses from the Social Science and Humanities programs would have to be seen as inconsistent with such a commitment. So also would the Business Administration program's decision to allow as many as five "free" electives, while encouraging students to take as many courses as possible in their major area. Such decisions were based on the assumption that there was no need for additional general education courses at the upper-division level because students had already met their general education requirements prior to admission. However, such requirements were often satisfied by any number of courses whose contents and goals had little to do with the aims of general education. For the Engineering Technology major, the number of Humanities and Social Science courses required for admission could be as few as two for those with an associate degree, and as many as seven for those transferring from a four-year college. An incoming student might have experienced a smattering of unrelated general education courses, such as music or art appreciation, literature surveys, surveys of Western civilization and the like, but not a series of courses which tried to integrate knowledge into some broader intellectual framework.

The reasons why the various programs chose to limit the number of electives are not difficult to understand. Students entering the last two years of their baccalaureate education could not long delay the specific courses needed for employment or for professional certification. With the costs of an education escalating every year, students were concerned about employment. Upper-division schools were designed to meet that concern. For many of Capitol's students, especially for many of the Engineering Technology and Business Administration students, college was to be the first step toward social and economic security. Reisman and Jencks' observation about prospective engineers applies to many of the students at our campus: "[They] are first-generation collegians who tend to view college in very narrowly vocational terms and tend to be aggressively hostile to liberal arts subjects, learning for its own sake and other presumed by-products of snobbery."[14] When the pursuit of a college education means a student will be mired in debt by the time he or she accepts a first job, the value of that education is more likely to be weighted in cost-benefit terms. The result of such a value judgment is that general education courses or interdisciplinary courses with a heavy reading requirement are not seen as having any practical value. General education proponents have had to face that argument and have learned to accept the compromises offered by faculty members and administrators who hold the middle ground between liberal and utilitarian education.

The advising policy at Capitol also contributed to the confusion over appropriate general education goals for this campus. Capitol's faculty adopted the view that students are best served when they have the freedom to choose courses that interest them. Most advisors try to strike a balance between recommending some of the interdisciplinary courses offered in the Humanities and Social Sciences and permitting the student to choose his own electives. But such a policy contradicts the view that general education goals are the chief concern of the institution because the student's freedom of choice may allow him to avoid general education courses entirely. While not wishing to abridge personal freedom, it is clear that some limitation of course choices should have been undertaken if Capitol was to be consistent with its mission. That was implicit in the design of the required general core courses. When the core was dropped, one of the principal means of achieving general education goals was lost. The institution had failed to develop a coherent plan for general education or a means of integrating the various courses in order to provide a common intellectual experience for its students.

Looking back over the past fifteen years, the problems faced by Capitol's faculty and administrators no longer seem unique. Many of the experiments that were tried were bound to fail because there were no models of upper-division campuses for us to emulate. Programs and experiments at Harvard, Chicago, or Minnesota could not be adapted to this institution.[15] Even though the campus mission statement was vague, each program had a specific responsibility to be innovative and interdisciplinary. Most tried to be so, especially in the early years (1966-1972) when each program group was an autonomous entity whose chairman reported directly to the Dean of the Faculty. By 1972, however, the programs had been organized into three divisions in order to streamline the management structure. Those divisions were split into six in 1978 to increase efficiency and to reflect more accurately the order of affairs. The academic reorganization plan clarified both the degree and service programs offered at Capitol and reflected the new Provost's desire to share campus governance with the faculty. At the same time, a new master plan was written to prepare the campus for the '80s. All of these changes were part of the process of giving the campus a new image and redefining its mission in Central Pennsylvania.

This brief review of the campus history and of its attempts to design a general core provides the background necessary for understanding the specific programs discussed in the next section. I believe that this historical introduction shows why the faculty chose to develop strong departmental programs rather than battle the issue of a limited number of required core courses for all students. As William Carlos Williams described his own efforts in writing a modern epic, Capitol's faculty needed:

> To make a start
> out of particulars
> and make them general, rolling
> up the sum by defective means.[16]

The failure to resolve the general education issue was not the result of ill will, disciplinarity ethnocentricity or of a half-hearted commitment to innovative education. A coherent plan for the campus could not be developed until the individual programs had been designed and until the relationship between the main campus and Capitol had been clarified. Both of those problems have been solved. As I will show in the next section, the faculty did find a way to develop new programs that were interdisciplinary and laid the groundwork for a reconsideration of general education as the campus confronts the challenge of changing from a term to a semester system in September of 1983.

Interdisciplinary Programs in the Social Sciences and Humanities

By the time the idea of the general core was discarded as unworkable, each of the academic programs had already designed specific core courses for its own majors. Most of the faculty involved in planning those courses had a strong interest in interdisciplinary studies, but were aware that the "goal of creating current-day Leonardos who are competent in all science" would lead to "a shallowness, a lowest common denominator breadth, an absence of that profound specialization

41

which is essential to scientific productivity."[17] Capitol's faculty avoided grandiose goals. The individual programs had decided that they could provide an overview of the various fields within a general subject area without deluding themselves into believing that such courses could ever encompass all that a student might need to know.

The Social Science and Humanities programs adopted core requirements in 1967. The Social Science faculty did so because they were guided by a significant body of literature suggesting that interdisciplinary Social Science courses were necessary not only for the universities, but also for students entering the various professions. Most of that literature argued for the desirability of a holistic view of Social Science. The disciplines or specialities shared a terminology and a subject matter. No single field possessed the means of justifying its isolation from the others or of testing the validity of its findings. To put the matter bluntly:

> Formulations about intergroup relations or leader-follower patterns, or power relations cannot be one thing when taught in a department of psychology and another thing when taught in a sociology department, and still another in a political science department, if any one of the disciplines in question claims validity for its formulations.[18]

The institutionalization of the Social Sciences had led to a fragmentation of the whole Social Science enterprise rather than an integration of its constituent disciplines with the other branches of knowledge on which they depend. As Muzafer Sherif argued in 1969:

> Failure to recognize the common and overlapping problems has led each of the social disciplines to preoccupation with minutiae and technicalities within its boundaries and to the avoidance of validity issues. Their disciplinary ethnocentrisms are encouraged by the structure of universities and professional societies.[19]

These views were instrumental in determining the organization of the Social Science program at Capitol. For example, in 1968 the new Psychosocial Science option was designed as an interdisciplinary program. In practice, that meant that the courses would draw upon social psychology, anthropology, sociology, and other fields in order to introduce the student to the theory and methodology of the field. Such courses were required before the student could proceed with specialized courses or field work. These courses were not a rehash of the introductory courses a student might have taken at the associate degree level, though some overlap became inevitable. The emphasis was on the relationships among the disciplines and not on their individual contents. This view reflected the belief that, given the limited number of faculty involved and the interdisciplinary ideals of the program, the only realistic approach to specialization was to select the material that every professional should know and to offer only that material in the formal course of study. Social Science students were given sufficient preparation for graduate work or for immediate employment in human services, business, public administration or industry. Preparing students for specific careers is not generally considered one of the primary goals of a liberal arts or humanistic education. Broader goals which develop a student's awareness and understanding of history and creativity, of literature and the arts, and of the value of pursuing those subjects throughout life are the typical goals mentioned most often in discussions of the role of the Humanities in higher education. These goals are acceptable for a four-year college, but a Humanities program in an upper-division institution has to adapt itself to more practical and justifiable goals. In 1966, Robert Altman warned that:

> If upper-division institutions choose to concentrate on liberal arts programs to the exclusion of other forms of baccalaureate education, they run the risk of failing not only to serving growing societal needs, but also to draw [sic] sufficient enrollment to ensure continued efficient operation.[20]

Capitol had no need of such a warning because the Humanities program was never envisioned as the one most likely to produce large enrollments. Early enrollment patterns fulfilled Altman's prediction that "future upper-division institutions will probably place less emphasis than before on the liberal arts degree and increasingly greater emphasis on the newly developing Bachelor of Technology degree or its equivalent."[21]

The Humanities program at Capitol has always had a service function, but it has also had majors of its own and a desire to be as innovative in its curriculum as any of the other programs. That desire was reflected in the options Humanities students could select. Since the mid-seventies, the most attractive options have been American Studies, Multi-Media Journalism, and Humanities-Business. Although each of those options was established for different reasons, the net benefit for the program was a small but stable enrollment of about 100 students.

Humanities was conceived as an interdisciplinary program because most of the faculty felt that their particular specialties were intellectually confining. As the number of staff increased during the period from 1969 to 1972, careful attention was given to the selection of individuals who could function as "one-person" departments. The reason for this was two-fold. First, the Humanities program would never be able to branch out into the traditional departments common to liberal arts colleges. Enrollment predictions and economic conditions dictated that the campus should not plan to duplicate programs offered by nearby colleges. We would not, for example, establish a studio arts program because the Harrisburg Area Community College already had an excellent facility and cooperation between the two institutions was being explored as early as 1974. Second, the Humanities program was not designed to produce specialists, but to emphasize interdisciplinarity as a means of helping students discover relationships among works of art, in specific historical periods, on the one hand, and investigating the methods common to all humanistic disciplines, on the other. Some concepts, such as periods or period-styles, can be approached only from a multidisciplinary viewpoint. With this rationale in mind, courses in philosophy, music, theatre, French studies, and art history were taught by individual specialists selected because they could teach several courses in their respective fields. Most of them had had some training--or at least a strong interest in--a second discipline and each had demonstrated a desire to pursue problems and issues outside his or her research interests. In fact, many set aside those specialized research interests for some time in order to prepare to teach a wide range of courses, give guest-lectures, experiment with team-teaching techniques, and assist in the planning of the Humanities core courses. They did so because they shared the conviction that:

> The problems that the Humanities attempt to solve
> are rooted in the deepest needs and perplexities
> of the human person who finds himself a member of
> a long tradition, when he searches for his own
> identity, faces the challenges of communal exis-
> tence, seeks to ground meaning and value in a world

that is much broader than the limits of his own
personal horizon and tries to make a positive contribution to the dialogue between himself and his
contemporaries.[22]

An example drawn from my first experiences as a
new staff member in Humanities will illustrate the
validity of that conviction. While we often discussed
the meaning of poetry, novels or drama in our consideration of the content of particular courses, many of us
wondered how such questions applied to music, painting,
or architecture. What does a musical phrase mean?
Music, by its very nature, is a non-verbal art. Though
it is commonly believed that music expresses something,
few are the musicians who can or will discuss such
questions. When they do, it is seldom done with any of
the precision used by colleagues in literature or art
history.

Those concerns might seem elitist from an out-
sider's point of view or from the vantage point of a
Humanities student concerned about future employment.
But we persisted in our concern with such questions because the answers would lead to an evaluation of what
we were teaching and why we used particular teaching
methods. There is little sense trying to perceive relationships among the arts when one has no answer to
questions about the value of the arts in specific historical or social contexts. Our perseverance led to
the establishment in 1972 of the Master of Arts in
Humanities program which has served as a research lab
where fundamental questions about the nature of interdisciplinary study in the Humanities could be investigated. That graduate program has been a blessing in
many ways. Its greatest benefit to the undergraduate
curriculum was that it provided the faculty with an
intellectual environment in which we could experiment
with teaching techniques and course materials using the
typical methods of scholarly inquiry. The faculty
always believed that the interrelationships we hoped
to discuss with our udnergraduates could survive the
kind of scholarly scrutiny typical of graduate research
programs.

While the undergraduate and graduate programs have
been dependent on one another, the goals of the former
are quite different. They are a combination of general
education goals and of the more specific goals typical
of disciplinary education. The core of the undergraduate program is a three-course sequence called "The
Western Tradition." Several different arts and at

least as many disciplines are integrated into a historical survey of Western culture. The core is required for all Humanities students and is based on several assumptions about teaching and about the value of a humanistic education. These assumptions were not just a summary of faculty views, but the result of suggestions brought to our attention by students and by an advisory committee of local media representatives formed at the time the Multi-Media Journalism option was established. They were refined following an evaluation of the undergraduate program by Phyllis Bober, a distinguished art historian and then Dean of the Graduate School of Bryn Mawr.[23] Since the advisory committee was made up of individuals who would be the future employers of our students, we were gratified that they expected our graduates to have more than a passing familiarity with some of the masterpieces of Western culture. Most employers believed that they could provide the appropriate technical training for our students during required internships; only Capitol could provide the kind of intellectual training associated with a traditional liberal education. Practical reasons aside, the actual design of the core courses was guided by some of the following assumptions:

1) A common intellectual experience is valuable because it gives students the opportunity of reading, discussing, and writing about some materials drawn from several different arts and at least as many disciplines.

2) Certain masterworks serve as the primary sources in such courses. Students are trained in the critical use of sources and in evaluating the cultural contexts in which such examples were created.

3) Humanities education is not a mere survey of texts, a quick slide-show of famous painting or a single hearing of a piece of music. There is a methodology to humanistic inquiry which is not the exclusive possession of scholars, but the refining of the informal methods of criticism and evaluation commonly used in life.

4) Specialization in any one art or in its related discipline is necessary, but not to the extent that it ignores the context of history, culture, and life.

The last assumption illustrates how strongly we believed that specialized knowledge should be "acquired

46

in a context of inquiry rich in philosophical and methodological presuppositions."[24] Adapting all of those assumptions to the classroom might appear to burden a student with an impossible task. In actual practice, most of the faculty know that they are teaching students who have selected the Humanities for practical reasons. The Humanities-Business students, for example, want specific skills, but they also continue to seek the benefits of the general education offered in the Humanities. Similarly, most Multi-Media majors want specific training in writing, production, and all the rest of the skills needed in a technologically-oriented industry. These are certainly practical goals. Such goals cannot be divorced from the value judgments every reporter, editor, or producer makes with each piece he or she creates. Such judgments are part of the process of selecting evidence, evaluating it, and presenting it to an audience. The Western Tradition courses are organized with reference to such goals. While each of the options provides specific training for its majors, all Humanities majors share the experiences of coming to grips with history and the way in which the history of culture and the arts is written.

The Western Tradition courses differ from the "Great Books" approach because none of them is limited to literature and because none of the instructors considers the few great books that we do use in isolation from their historical and social contexts. Those contexts are the subjects of the other disciplines that are incorporated into courses with the emphasis on the discipline necessary for interpretation. It is obvious that few humanists can consider enough of the evidence necessary for anything more than a general understanding of an unfamiliar culture. Our approach is modest. Though the number of works studied must sometimes be small, the method of studying them can be quite challenging when the various arts and disciplines are combined into a coherent approach to cultural history.

Each of the courses deals with a specific time period and with several cultures within that period. The first includes ancient classical civilizations, the second, the Middle Ages and Renaissance, and the third covers the period from 1600 to 1900.[25] Although all of the faculty agree in principle on the assumptions stated above, each is encouraged to conduct his or her classes differently. There have been no standard syllabi and the various methods of teaching reflect the diversity of approaches to interdisciplinary courses reported in the literature.[26] Some use a scientific approach; that is, they select primary works from a variety of media and those examples serve as the basis for the practice of a humanistic methodology. Others emphasize a historical approach in which the consideration of a chronological narrative is enriched by the use of primary sources and the examples chosen serve as aesthetic guideposts revealing the relationships between history, art, and life. Finally, a few--myself among them--believe that a true interdisciplinary program cannot be achieved unless there is an integration of the various arts and their related disciplines into a teaching method that combines primary works, the historical narrative, and relevant social or cultural history.

Each of the approaches described carries with it its own particular problems. Whatever the approach, the courses are difficult to teach. The process of selection must be rigorous and time must be spent helping students appreciate what they see, read, and hear. The student body is so diverse, their cultural backgrounds so different, that the emphasis on a scholarly methodology can lead to a quick disenchantment with the whole sequence of courses. As Hans Flexner has argued: "The manner in which knowledge is obtained is by no means always the most effective way to teach."[27] All those who have taught the core courses have come to realize that our teaching must demonstrate that learning can be intellectually and emotionally rewarding. That statement applies to the teaching of Humanities at any institution. At an upper-division college, it is an article of faith. The reason for choosing primary sources is to bring the student into personal contact with the works that scholars write and think about and to help the student experience these works directly. We may take it as self-evident that Plato, Vergil, Dante, Shakespeare or Goethe are great writers, that Bach, Beethoven or Stravinsky are great composers, but our students must discover that for themselves. If our methodology gets in the way of that discovery, it has obscured and hindered the student's perception of human creativity. The Western Tradition courses should help him understand himself and the world in which he lives by challenging, persuading, and encouraging him to consider that past as part of a living heritage.

All our experiments with the graduate and undergraduate programs at this campus have taught us that interdisciplinary research and teaching are different things. The criteria for judging these endeavors are different. If we have confused these tasks in the past, the current situation reveals that the lesson had best

be remembered because this campus cannot resist the
trend toward career education. What our history has
taught us is that we must demonstrate that preparation
for a vocation does not preclude the nurturing of an
avocation. That point has been made clear to us by the
increasing numbers of Business Administration and Engineering Technology students who elect the Western
Tradition courses or some of the interdisciplinary
courses in the arts, music, and American studies. Those
students are not always interested in learning a humanistic methodology, but are seeking the experience of
reading great literature as well as learning about the
other arts. That increase, while not large at present,
is due in part to the fact that course descriptions
circulate to all advisors and are available in several
campus locations. Many students also discuss their
schedules with the Humanities faculty during the pre-
registration period and seem to be willing to take
courses that will satisfy their curiosity or special
interests.

The pattern just described provides the best evidence that maintaining general education courses at the
upper-division level is an obligation. It also suggests
that the campus position on academic advising should be
strengthened, but should not restrict a student's freedom so long as he or she chooses some courses that fulfill the general education goals of the campus. Small
groups of students seem to be selecting such courses
without strong sermons of encouragement. If this emerging pattern persists, the faculty would do well to consider it as a way of recommitting the campus to the
task of incorporating general education goals into a
variety of courses in the Humanities which may seem to
serve Humanities majors only. During a recent address
at the University-wide General Education Conference, the
Provost of the University, Dr. Edward D. Eddy, argued
that:

> In approaching general education, land-grant uni-
> versities [Penn State is such an institution] have
> attempted to tie together the purposes of "making
> a living" and "making a life." The land-grant
> ideal clearly is the union of general and profes-
> sional education not just in the same university
> but in the same classroom. The issue is not the
> end but the means; not why, but how.[28]

The Humanities faculty are committed to unifying
general and professional education through interdisciplinary studies. The various options, American Studies,

Humanities-Business, and the Multi-Media Journalism options in particular, do just that. Rather than designing new courses or trying to revive the interdisciplinary core, the best solution in achieving the ideal mentioned by Dr. Eddy will be to demonstrate to our students and colleagues that the ideal can be realized at this campus. This solution recognizes the specific needs of this campus and may well apply to other upper-division institutions concerned with the role of the Humanities in their curriculum. Sometimes it seems that the greatest problems of communication in an institution are internal. At Capitol, the Humanities faculty have taken initiatives to introduce new faculty to the services provided by the program and to orient new students to the opportunities for creative activities and exciting learning on this campus. Humanities programs at this campus and many others have a much better chance of survival if we all use our communication skills more and respond effectively to the challenges of defending the value of general education courses at our respective institutions.

Graduate Education at the Capitol Campus

Graduate work has always been an integral part of the campus mission. Even though graduate education is not separately budgeted and though few of the typical benefits (teaching assistantships, research assistantships, fellowships) are available to graduate students, the possibilities for research and the challenges of working in interdisciplinary programs were instrumental in attracting faculty. Most of the staff hold the Ph.D. and are appointed to the graduate faculty on a University-wide basis. There is therefore no question of equal status with respect to the faculty at the main campus. Since all of the faculty also teach in the undergraduate programs, they must make time for their own research and writing. Capitol's faculty have with no little cost been able to find the time for research and funding statistics show that support for faculty projects has increased significantly since the graduate programs were established. The amount of funded research has grown from $53,000 in 1973 to $623,000 in 1979-80. A major proportion of that support is provided by the University which has made a notable commitment to sponsoring research at Capitol. Particularly useful in this respect, are small grants (under $1,000) which are used to help junior faculty with the cost of research and travel. All of these factors demonstrate the importance placed on continued faculty growth through scholarship and publication.

The cooperation between Capitol and graduate programs at the main campus began with the Master of Engineering degree in 1968-69. While that degree is still under the control and supervision of the College of Engineering, Capitol's other degree programs have achieved a greater degree of autonomy. Graduate studies must still be approved by the University's graduate school, but that office has shown a willingness to allow Capitol to experiment with a variety of approaches to graduate work. In many ways, Capitol's location makes it ideally suited for such work because, unlike the main campus, it is close to the state capitol and surrounded by a major metropolitan area that has grown significantly since 1966.

Certain graduate programs, such as those in American Studies, Humanities, and Education, tended to grow out of interdisciplinary undergraduate programs. Others, such as the Psychosocial program in Community Psychology, were linked to the mission of practical, urban-oriented and interdisciplinary courses of study. That program has a forty-five credit degree requirement (thirty credits is the campus average) and nine of those credits must be in field work. The student is not required to write a traditional thesis, but must write a summary of the field experience and defend that essay in order to graduate. Like the other graduate programs at this campus, the Psychosocial program is tailored to the individual student's needs and appropriate courses are offered in Public Administration, Regional Planning and Behavioral Science in order to stress a multidisciplinary view of community health work. What distinguishes this program from those in other graduate schools is the emphasis on practical experience, on a multidisciplinary approach to problems and on the consolidation of relevant subject matter into a few interdisciplinary courses. The program was one of the first to be described in the literature on interdisciplinary experiments in the 70s and Donald Campbell's prediction about the potential success of the program was correct. He noted that:

> Capitol Campus will start out with no budgetary departments within the Division of Social Science. If they [sic] forgo the temptation of turning out "well-rounded social scientists" and allow as narrow a specialization as any traditional department, but with the freedom for novel narrowness, the training program should be successful.[29]

The Psychosocial program has been very successful.

It is an example of how an innovative program can reconcile new ideas, teaching techniques and interdisciplinary courses with community needs and with a student's
plans for a specific career. There may be some regret
that all but a few students are not "well-rounded-social
scientists" or that they may not be interested in
research for its own sake. Given the limitations of the
institution, they are at least well prepared. The program can demonstrate a high rate of acceptance at other
graduate schools for those students desiring work at
the doctoral level.

The Master's program in Public Administration
offers a degree for administrators in state and local
government, for students seeking careers in health-ser-
vice professions and for those beginning new careers in
mid-life. Many of the students are already employed
and need the degree for job advancement. Like the other
graduate programs, this one also has several internship
programs, the newest of which is for research associates
who will work with the Pennsylvania Senate. A doctoral
program in Political Science has been approved recently
and will be offered in cooperation with the Department
of Political Science at University Park.

The Business Administration program has in recent
years acknowledged the demand for a traditional M.B.A.
because of the growing prestige of that degree. Since
graduate students are drawn from the large undergraduate
program (38 percent of the student population as of
Fall, 1981) and since the Business Division is actively
involved in seeking accreditation, it has been forced
to move toward a less innovative curriculum. By and
large, the programs which have most to win or lose in
the judgments of outside accrediting associations have
had the hardest time creating and maintaining innovative programs. In some professions, innovation is a
liability and the academic world must compromise with
the demands of the marketplace when training students
in various business professions.

While external demands have limited the range of
innovation in the Engineering and Business Divisions,
the graduate programs in Humanities and American Studies have faced no such constraints. The Humanities
program is one of the most flexible because it is competency-based,[30] that is, it requires specific levels
of competence in two or more disciplines, rather than
demanding a prescribed number of courses. It also
offers the student the option of completing a "creative
production" instead of a traditional thesis. The com-

52

petency requirement means that students are expected to demonstrate: a familiarity with the basic tools of disciplinary and interdisciplinary research, an ability to criticize and evaluate works of art in various media, and, finally, they must synthesize the results of their research and generalize about the interrelationships among the arts. The "creative production" is somewhat similar to those required in M.F.A. programs, but the production must be accompanied by a critical paper demonstrating the student's scholarly abilities. Throughout the period of graduate study, Humanities students are guided by a supervisory committee whose chairperson sees to it that the student acquires the skills necessary for continued work in the program.

The interdisciplinary program in Humanities stresses the common procedures used by the various disciplines, while at the same time respecting the differences among the various arts. Although breadth cannot be achieved in the M.A. program, students learn that the techniques needed for gaining some knowledge of many different fields can be synthesized. In some respects, this approach represents an intensive effort to liberalize graduate education at the master's level by emphasizing the student's acquisition of the analytical and critical techniques common to several disciplines. Disciplinary education is not discouraged because a student must be competent in some particular field. Students, like their faculty mentors, are subject to the constant review of their peers. That review process includes one of the criticisms most frequently encountered in evaluations of interdisciplinary studies.

Interdisciplinary work will almost always face charges of dilettantism, and interdisciplinarians, in order to maintain themselves in a disciplinary environment, will be pressed to continually prove their credentials as disciplinarians. Their interdisciplinary work can only be pursued part-time giving further weight to any criticism of dilettantism.[31]

There is a great deal of skepticism on the part of traditional disciplinarians about interdisciplinary, competency-based education. The Humanities faculty at Capitol believe that, after ten years of working with such an approach, students can be trained to guard themselves against naive reductionism when appropriate research skills are coupled with a critical evaluation of the limitations of inter-art analogies. Even if our students eventually decide to major in a specific field,

53

the benefit of the interdisciplinary approach will give
them a better understanding of the problems peculiar to
that field. An example will clarify our view.

Many of our incoming students seem to believe that
artists create because of a desire or need for self-
expression. Yet the theory of expression is one of
many alternative aesthetic theories. An inter-art, or
better, an interdisciplinary investigation of the theory
and of examples drawn from literature, painting, and
music reveals that the theory is an inadequate explana-
tion of artistic creativity and is virtually useless in
explaining the meaning of works of art. Without the
experience of considering the differences among works
of art and the various attempts to interpret them, students and faculty alike miss the opportunity to raise
deeper questions about creativity and significance in
the arts.

Interdisciplinary approaches to analysis and criticism can also illustrate how individual disciplines
are the products of their time and of specific critical
ideologies. Take, for example, Meyer Abrams' objective
theory of art. That theory and the method of criticism
derived from it have been adapted to the analysis of
music and to the criticism of modern painting.[32] Most
of those using the theory are unaware of the fact that
the theory is an autotelic one, i.e., it assumes that
art objects are autonomous entities following their own
rules. Such a method effectively isolates the work of
art from its historical contexts, its traditions, and,
most important, from all but the most perceptive of
audiences. These examples illustrate the sources of
our dissatisfaction with the limitations of some disciplines. Although the Humanities faculty are concerned
with such questions, most of the group remain committed
to a discipline because of the organization of their
respective professions. Nevertheless, they have retained their interest in interdisciplinary studies and
that is the reason why the program has outlived many
others founded on the same assumptions. As Wolfram
Zwoboda noted in 1970:

> The prospects for interdisciplinarity as such,
> within the context and as a permanent feature of
> American higher education, do not seem altogether
> hopeful. There are to be considered the dynamics
> of institutionalization, which are overwhelmingly
> disciplinary and which have transformed previous
> potential interdisciplinarities as diverse as edu-

cation, philosophy, and social psychology into disciplines proper. Interdisciplinary efforts grafted onto existing institutions will likely remain temporary or isolated phenomena, most either being terminated or becoming absorbed into disciplinary structures.[33]

The program at Capitol has outlasted such predictions because it has considered its constituents and because the campus itself has tried to retain useful academic innovations even during times of dire predictions about future enrollment. One of the most important features of the Humanities program's concern with the needs of its students is the internship in junior-college teaching which is available to qualified students. Our students have been placed in several community colleges in Pennsylvania and their practical experiences have usually led to permanent employment. Many secondary school teachers have taken advantage of the program in order to enrich their own teaching and to introduce interdisciplinary work into the secondary school curriculum. Other students have gone on to doctoral work elsewhere. Because the Humanities program addresses itself to the study of inter-art analogies and the interdependence of the various disciplines, most of our students have viewed the program as one which fulfills many personal goals, rather than one whose practical benefits are immediately applicable to their particular career plans.

Graduate work in the Humanities has been the subject of constant faculty evaluation, has been monitored carefully by the Graduate School at University Park, and has benefited from the recommendations of the N.E.H. consultant's report referred to earlier. Although the competency-based approach was experimental in 1972, it has proven its value in the face of the Graduate School's later insistence on a minimum thirty-credit requirement for the M.A. in Humanities. The principal value is that students have shown that they can learn the basic techniques of various disciplines with faculty guidance and that they do not need formal course work to do so. In a very real sense, they learn that education and scholarship involve a considerable amount of individual initiative and are encouraged to follow the lead of respected scholars who have ventured outside the security of their own respective fields.

The American Studies graduate program is equally interdisciplinary and practical in its approach to educating students for particular career goals. Courses in that program are staffed by faculty from the Behavioral Science and Humanities Divisions. Historians, social scientists (principally anthropologists, psychologists, and folklorists) as well as art and music historians are involved in teaching a variety of courses that emphasize an interdisciplinary approach to American Studies. Graduate students can take advantage of a number of internships in museums, historical commissions, and various governmental agencies. The American Studies program is unique in the ways that its courses integrate art, architecture, and music as well as social and political history within the general context of American history.

The graduate programs have helped Capitol develop a positive image in the community. Although most of them are designed to meet diverse community needs, they are only a part of the wide range of services offered; for example, an Institute of Regional Planning, a Small Business Development Center, and the Pennsylvania Data Center of the U.S. Census Bureau. While the majority of graduate students come from within traveling distance of the campus, an increasing number of foreign students have chosen Capitol's programs in recent years. The future development of the campus seems to lie in an extension of its mission statewide in order to accommodate students from four-year institutions and to broaden the range of its services to business and industry.

Future Prospects for General Education at Capitol

This review of Capitol's history indicates how this campus differs from other institutions. Capitol has had notable success with most of its innovative and interdisciplinary programs. Changing conditions have led to a decrease in the faculty's interest in innovation for its own sake and to a consideration of the practical questions of adapting the original mission to predictions about student enrollment in the 80s. Sixty-three percent of the current student body of 2,523 (Fall, 1981) are enrolled in the Business Administration and Engineering Technology Divisions. The popularity of those programs has led to very critical screening procedures and to an increase in the minimum grade-point average required for admission. Each of those divisions has already applied for or is seriously considering accreditation by professional agencies. The enrollments in other programs are not so encouraging, even though they remain stable at present. Enrollment is always an important concern because of the untraditional character of an upper-division college. As this report indicates, Capitol cannot offer all the services of a four-year college, nor can it offer the variety of programs common at such institutions. It is in fact a unique institution with strong and successful academic programs. Aggressive recruiting and a rededication to the service mission of the campus will undoubtedly be the keys to future growth.

At the beginning of this report, I mentioned that an integrated curriculum was important to the faculty and administrators who were planning the various academic programs. As this campus faces the calendar change in 1983, the issue of an integrated curriculum is again under consideration. With that important issue in mind, I believe that Capitol's uniqueness has been both a benefit and a burden. Free to develop new programs, the faculty responded with courses which served the needs of students seeking a professional education. Other academic programs were designed with broader goals and were concerned with the idea of "making a life" as well as "making a living." Some of the graduate programs were capstones for undergraduate education, while others were established to serve specific community and student needs. All of the programs provided sufficient flexibility for students with diverse educational goals and expectations to plan their own academic programs. Taken in sum, the desire to provide so many services to so many different kinds of students pushed the idea of an integrated curriculum into the background. Nevertheless, a few programs were able to retain a commitment to general education goals and most of the means of achieving those goals, such as courses, programs, and faculty, were available for students who sought such an education.

In conclusion, I believe that four steps can be taken to make general education a part of the academic mission of this campus. They are: (1) an innovative adaptation of existing interdisciplinary courses and the development of new ones which emphasize general education in the context of contemporary issues, (2) better accessibility to information about the courses, programs, and options currently available at this campus by improving internal communication between academic divisions, (3) greater awareness on the part of students and faculty of the differences between Capitol and other types of institutions together with the limitations imposed by those differences, and (4) responsible academic advising to insure that some general education requirements are met by every student. The last suggestion should be consistent with the campus policy of giving the student some freedom in meeting degree re-quirements.

Capitol Campus is a different kind of educational institution. It is a unique part of a twenty-campus system of a major land-grant University. The campus had to establish an identity different from the other units of the University. Having accomplished that task with great administrative and faculty effort, Capitol must proceed into the 80s with a clearer sense of its academic mission. Questions such as the role of the Humanities at an upper-division institution, the selection of electives, the articulation of relation-ships between community colleges and associate degree programs, as well as the relationship between the various graduate programs and the service mission of the campus, are likely to remain perennial concerns. Now that Capitol has reached its fifteenth year, the goal of achieving an integrated curriculum remains a task for those who will plan the next phase of its academic development.

William J. Mahar
Humanities and Music

Footnotes

[1]For a history of the origins of Capitol Campus, see Robert Altman, The Upper-Division College (San Francisco: Jossey-Bass, 1970), 149-155. Additional information on the campus can be found in the booklet published by the University for the Fifteenth Anniversary Convocation (Nov. 11, 1981) and available from the campus relations office.

[2]Altman, p. 152.

[3]The students at Capitol include junior college transfers from four-year colleges and from other campuses of the University, returning women, and students of various ages admitted via CLEP. The average student age is 27.

[4]For a discussion of various models, see Harry Finestone and Michael F. Shugrue, eds., Prospects for the 70's: English Departments and Multidisciplinary Study (New York: MLA, 1973); Muzafer Sherif and Carolyn Sherif, eds., Interdisciplinary Relationships in the Social Sciences (Chicago: Aldine, 1969); Joseph J. Kockelmans, ed., Interdisciplinarity in Higher Education (University Park, P.A.: Penn State, 1979); Lewis B. Mayhew and Patrick J. Ford, Changing the Curriculum (San Francisco: Jossey-Bass, 1971). Also George A. Morgan, "A New Interdisciplinary Curriculum," in G. Kerry Smith, ed., New Teaching, New Learning: Current Issues in Higher Education (San Francisco: Jossey-Bass, 1971).

[5]Vincent C. Kavaloski, "Interdisciplinary Education and Humanistic Aspiration: A Critical Reflection," in Kockelmans, Interdisciplinarity, 224-225, pp. 224-243. Quoted excerpt abridged for clarity. Throughout this essay, interdisciplinary is to be taken in a generic sense for any courses or approaches which utilize the tools or results of one or more disciplines.

[6]Daniel Bell, The Reforming of General Education: The Columbia Experience in its National Setting (New York: Columbia, 1966), p. 180.

[7]Bell, p. 257.

[8]Bell, p. 180.

[9]Forrest H. Armstrong, "Faculty Development through Interdisciplinarity," Journal of General Education, XXXII, no. 1 (Spring, 1980), 52-63, p. 54.

[10]Jerry G. Gaff and others, The Cluster College (San Francisco: Jossey-Bass, 1970), p. 43.

[11]Frederick Rudolph, Curriculum: A History of the Undergraduate Course of Study Since 1636 (San Francisco, Jossey-Bass, 1978), p. 248.

[12]Gerald Grant, "The Overoptioned Curriculum," in Toward the Restoration of the Liberal Arts Curriculum: A Rockefeller Foundation Conference (New York: The Rockefeller Foundation, 1979), 26-36, p. 34.

[13]Study results quoted and summarized in Arthur Levine, Handbook on Undergraduate Curriculum (San Francisco: Jossey-Bass, 1978), p. 36.

[14]Christopher Jencks and David Reisman, The Academic Revolution (Garden City, N.Y.: Doubleday, 1968), p. 229.

[15]See, "Curriculum Highlights of the Past: 1900-1964," in Levine, Handbook, 344-365. For a sample of reactions to the Harvard general education program, see Bell, Reforming, 183-190, and Barry O'Connell, "Where Does Harvard Lead Us?" in Toward the Restoration of the Liberal Arts, 59-76.

[16]William Carlos Williams, Paterson (New York: New Directions, 1963), 5 vols. in one, I, II.

[17]Donald Campbell, "Ethnocentrism of Disciplines and the Fish-Scale Model of Omniscience," in Muzafer Sherif, Interdisciplinary Relationships, 328-348, p. 339.

[18]Muzafer Sherif and Carolyn Sherif, "Interdisciplinary Coordination as a Validity Check," in Sherif, Interdisciplinary Relationships, 3-20, p. 5.

[19]Muzafer Sherif, "Crossdisciplinary Coordination in the Social Sciences," In Kockelmans, Interdisciplinarity, 197-223, p. 197.

[20]Altman, Upper-Division College, p. 175.

[21]Altman, p. 170.

[22] Joseph J. Kockelmans, "Science and Discipline: Some Historical and Critical Reflections," in Kockelmans, Interdisciplinarity, 11-48, p. 39.

[23] Phyllis Pray Bober, Final Report: Consultancy to Humanities Program (N.E.H. Grant No. H-24-186, Oct. 27, 1976). Copies available from the Humanities Division, Capitol Campus.

[24] Bell, Reforming, p. 279.

[25] The Humanities Division has recently approved an interdisciplinary American Studies course as a continuation of the Western Tradition series in order to integrate the study of Western culture with the American experience and to deal with contemporary issues in American history.

[26] Hans Flexner and Gerald Hauser, "Interdisciplinary Programs in the United States: Some Paradigms," in Kockelmans, Interdisciplinarity, 328-350. See also Levine, Handbook, 18-19, and Interdisciplinarity: Problems in Teaching and Research (Paris: OECD, 1972).

[27] Hans Flexner, "The Curriculum, the Disciplines, and Interdisciplinarity in Higher Education: Historical Perspective," in Kockelmans, Interdisciplinarity, 93-122, p. 117.

[28] Quoted in Capitol Campus Currents [an alumni newsletter], II, no. 9 (Feb. 10, 1983), p. 4.

[29] Campbell, "Ethnocentrism," in Sherif, Interdisciplinary Relationships, p. 340.

[30] Levine, Handbook, 409-413 reports on the competency-based undergraduate program begun at Sterling College in 1972. While the methods of evaluating competencies at Sterling differ from those used at Capitol, both institutions have had similar difficulties in implementing the competency-based approach.

[31] Wolfram Zwoboda, "Disciplines and Interdisciplinarity: A Historical Perspective," In Kockelmans, Interdisciplinarity, 49-92, p. 80.

[32] For a criticism of the methods of musical analysis, see Joseph Kerman, "How We Got into Analysis and How to Get Out," In Critical Inquiry, VII, no. 2 (Winter, 1980), 311-331; for the visual arts, Leo

Steinberg, "The Eye is a Part of the Mind," In Other Criteria: Confrontations with Twentieth-Century Art (New York: Oxford, 1972), 289-306.

[33]Zwoboda, "Disciplines," in Kockelmans, Interdisciplinarity, pp. 82-83.

THE INTEGRATED LIBERAL STUDIES PROGRAM
UNIVERSITY OF WISCONSIN, MADISON

The Recent Crisis

In April of 1979, acting on the advice of his Academic Planning Committee, the Dean of the College of Letters and Science decided to terminate the Integrated Liberal Studies Program (ILS), a two-year general education sequence that has operated at the University of Wisconsin since 1948 and which therefore was one of the oldest continuing programs of its kind in the nation. Noting that ILS had rendered a unique service to the College and had provided some of its most innovative teaching, Dean E. David Cronon commented on the program's performance in recent years and cited these reasons for his decision:

1) declining enrollment, particularly in the sophomore year;
2) lack of apparent faculty interest;
3) loss of a cohesive vision in the curriculum and consensus as to future direction.

However, the Faculty Senate of the College, meeting in November, recommended instead that ILS be reduced to a one-year freshman program and continued on an interim basis, pending further consideration. An ad-hoc committee (the third in a decade) was appointed by the Dean to evaluate the future of the troubled program.

At the same time, a small group of faculty who previously had not been involved in ILS volunteered to join several of the experienced faculty in developing new courses and restructuring the curriculum. When I became the Chairman in February, 1980, it was agreed that we would alter the basic structure of the program, that we would actively recruit additional colleagues from the tenured ranks, and that we would work closely with the new evaluating committee in drafting our proposals. In December, 1980, the committee reported to the Dean, endorsing our plan for a new Integrated Liberal Studies Program. We are now in the process of implementing that plan. ILS continues on an interim basis and will be re-evaluated in 1983-84.

What follows is a more detailed history of the program and an account of our attempt to redesign it. Because many of the difficulties that beset ILS in the

63

1970s were shared by interdisciplinary programs at other institutions, our experience may be of significance to educators elsewhere. Wisconsin is an interesting study in this regard. On more than one occasion questions have been raised regarding the mission of an interdisciplinary program, its internal organization, and its relation to the College of Letters and Science as a whole. As one of the major research centers in the nation, the University naturally promotes a structure most responsive to specialization through departments. How, then, to design a program of general education compatible with the characteristics of a large university dominated by its prestigious graduate school and pre-professional programs? In recent years the problem grew acute, but this issue has been a continuing one on the Madison campus for better than half a century.

The Meiklejohn Experimental College, 1927-1932

For this reason it may be useful to consider the problems facing ILS in light of past developments. To do so, we must begin in 1925. Those familiar with the history of general education in the United States may be curious as to the relation between the ILS program and the famous Meiklejohn Experimental College, which preceded it. It is true that the two programs are linked historically, but whereas they may have shared a common purpose (that of general education), in specific respects they were quite dissimilar.

Alexander Meiklejohn already had established a reputation as a controversial educator when he was invited by President Glenn Frank in 1925 to come to Wisconsin with the purpose of establishing a "college within a college" to experiment with educational policy. The "college" opened in 1927, charged with criticizing, at least implicitly, the university that housed it. The experiment featured special "outside" faculty imported by Meiklejohn to teach in the program; shared office space and dormitory accommodations for faculty and students; a segregated (and all-male) student population; tutorials instead of lectures; modules rather than semester sequences; a common reading list for the entire college; and policies regarding grading and attendance that differed markedly from standard practice. The chief and most radical aim of the experiment was to fuse together the intellectual and social activities of the students.

Meiklejohn's Philosophy

Meiklejohn believed that the purpose of education was to build intelligence, not to disseminate knowledge or professional skills. The college, he argued, should be "as much and as little interested in the making of scholars as it is in the making of bankers, legislators, grocers, or the followers of any other specialized occupation or profession."[1] He asserted also that "a college is a group of people, all of whom are reading the same books."[2] In effect, participants found themselves immersed in an intense, two-year theme course in which everyone studied a unified reading list focusing on the comparison between classical Greek and present day American society. The program was divided into six-week segments, during which students discussed government, economics, literature, the arts, and philosophy, with an aim toward "integrating" the material they read. Writing assignments were frequent. Provisions were made also for inclusion of the physical sciences in the curriculum. Meiklejohn estimated that students by the end of the sophomore year had completed the equivalent of 5 semester courses in economics, politics, and other social studies; 4½ semester courses of literature and the arts; 3½ semester courses of philosophy and religion; 3 semester courses of science; 1 semester course of general introduction to college work; and 3 semester courses of "special papers" (or independent study).[3] As an example of the latter, each student in 1928 was required to undertake an analysis of the political, economic, and cultural life of his home town, keeping in mind what he had learned about Athenian civilization.

Failure of the Experiment

At its peak, the Experimental College enrolled 155 students. According to the testimony of some of these graduates, the program was enormously stimulating. But the college also encouraged rivalry and dissension. Whatever were the fruits of Meiklejohn's experiment, the idea of a separate college with separate policies for a "special" group of undergraduates did not root well in Wisconsin soil. The college, as critics observed, attracted a larger proportion of out of state students than did other units at the University; there were free-thinkers, artists, a few socialists, and a visible Jewish population from the East. This cluster discomfited provincial constituencies on campus and in the state legislature. Too, certain students outside the program resented the fact that the Experimental college dispensed with the usual semester grades.

Personality also played a part in the college's demise. Although Meiklejohn won the loyalty of his students, he failed to forge reciprocal relations with his colleagues in other departments. His procedures--indeed, the very existence of the College--threatened to undermine departmental hegemony. Often where tact might have served, Meiklejohn barged ahead. For example, chairmen were asked to absorb Meiklejohn's faculty into their own departments and then to grant them release time to teach in the experimental program. More than a little resentment accompanied Meiklejohn's proposal to set salaries for his faculty at higher rates than those current in the regular departments. Finally --and above all--there were not many on campus who actually subscribed to his philosophy. As the Depression worsened, the perception grew that the College was an unaffordable luxury, and each year Meiklejohn's support decreased. In 1932, after a colorful half-decade during which Meiklejohn received more favorable notice outside the community than within it (which sometimes is the case with prophets), the Experimental College closed its doors.

The Integrated Liberal Studies Program, 1948-1979:
Founding

In the period of growth on the Madison campus following the Second World War, there arose considerable faculty interest in reviving the principle of general education, although the concept of a separate college based on the Meiklejohn model was now deemed undesirable. In this context ILS was established--sixteen years after the Meiklejohn experiment ended.[4] Following a general review of the Letters and Science curriculum, a committee appointed by Dean Mark Ingraham in 1946, chaired by Professor Frederick Ogg, proposed a two-year program that came to be called Integrated Liberal Studies. Its declared purpose was "to help students see the interrelationships between the various areas of specialization in which they and their teachers are immersed." The program was organized in 1947 and went into effect in 1948, chaired by Professor Robert Pooley of the Department of English. Initially enrollment was restricted to 300 students per class to encourage close contact and informal relations with the faculty. But these students did not constitute a group separate from the rest of the campus, and they were governed by normal university regulations. Many other features of the program owed their existence to the memory of the failed Experimental College. Courses were taught in the traditional way with lectures, examinations, and grades. The integrating theme was history, and the courses taken as follows:

First Year

Greek and Roman Culture (4 credits). Walter Agard, Paul MacKendrick.
Medieval and Renaissance Culture (3 credits). Gaines Post.
Early Man and His Society (3 credits). William W. Howells.
Transition to Industrial Society (4 credits). Robert Reynolds.
Physical Universe (6 credits). Arch Gerlach, Aaron Ihde.
English Composition (4 credits). Robert Pooley.

Second Year

European Culture, 1750-1850 (4 credits). Robert Pooley.
Recent American Culture (3 credits). Frederick Hoffman.
Modern Industrial Society (4 credits). James Early.
The International Scene (3 credits). Llewellyn Pfankuchen.
Biology (7 credits). C. Leonard Huskins, Lowell E. Noland.

The curriculum for the second year once again placed stress on social issues, but compared to the Meiklejohn curriculum, this emphasis was much reduced. Finally, to mark the program clearly as part of the College of Letters and Science, ILS adopted a departmental structure in conformity with normal college practice. A key provision was that its faculty were to be "borrowed" from other traditional or "home" departments.

Borrowed Faculty

In this way, the organizers of ILS addressed the problem of "outside faculty" that had proved so distressing under Meiklejohn. As far as could be seen, this policy was sound. However, no satisfactory mechanism was established to evaluate the work and teaching loads of borrowed faculty or to provide funds outside departmental budgets for merit increases or other faculty support; nor were reciprocal relationships established with the home departments regarding the important matters of promotion and/or nonretention. To this extent the new ILS program inherited Meiklejohn's dilemma. Later, failure to resolve these issues resulted in a pattern of disincentives for those faculty who might be interested in teaching in the program yet who naturally were concerned with normal progress in their careers.

Nevertheless, owing largely to the efforts of the original ILS faculty, many of whom had distinguished themselves in their respective fields, the program functioned with notable success, acclaim, and student interest for better than a generation. The founders had a clear vision of their goals and seemed spurred by their collective purpose. They met frequently for discussion and occasionally monitored each other's courses. By all accounts, the level of teaching in ILS was high. In addition, an active faculty-student social life developed in the 1940s. Lectures, coffee-hours, "firesides" in faculty homes, and other group events generated cohesion in the program. Obviously, these events reflected a willingness on the part of faculty members to devote a good portion of their time to ILS-related activities. In these years the program thrived.

Faculty Attrition

Only gradually did negative trends appear. In the mid-1960's, the generation of founding faculty reached retirement age (12 of the original 14 faculty had remained with the program from the start), and it proved difficult to replace them. Evidently their dedication had long sustained a system that was ill-designed for self-renewal. Those who did enter the program in the '60s labored against odds; for the first time faculty turnover was high. It then became necessary to recruit lecturers who were not regular tenure-track faculty, a situation that the founders of ILS had hoped to avoid. Later this problem was underscored by the case of a popular lecturer in ILS who, having no home department outside the program, could not be renewed. Graduate assistants were called upon to assume a higher proportion of teaching duties in the program; on this basis some administrators questioned the quality and level of instruction. It is difficult to assess the facts in this matter, but one pattern was definite: as senior faculty left, it became increasingly difficult to recruit full-time faculty from the home departments, which controlled the reward-system of the college. It became even more difficult to maintain the cohesive integration between courses that had characterized the program in the early years. Here and there excellent new courses were added, but often in a fashion tailored more to the interests of the volunteering instructor than to the overall concept of the curriculum. Thus, faculty attrition was the first indication of decline.

Enrollment Decline

A second negative trend was an alarming decline in student enrollment. About 200 freshmen entered the program in 1948, while a high of 415 enrolled in 1965. But throughout the late '60s and the '70s, the numbers fell, and precipitously in the sophomore year. Only a small percentage of the entering freshman class remained to complete the program, as evidenced in the following table:

TABLE 1

Approximate Enrollments in ILS, 1965-1979

Year entering UW	Freshman Sem. 1	Freshman Sem. 2	Sophomore Sem. 1	Sophomore Sem. 2
1965	415	327	137	129
1966	346	221	116	80
1967	266	186	86	73
1968	269	161	91	70
1969	230	140	89	61
1970	301	119	75	58
1971	172	123	83	65
1972	180	129	72	48
1973	171	106	63	42
1974	173	106	53	43
1975	186	107	45	43
1976	141	66	54	43
1977	176	121	68	26
1978	163	112	57	?
1979	168	79	--	--

Requirements as Deterrents

The relatively inflexible requirements of the program served as deterrents to enrollment. Students were
asked to commit themselves to 25 credits of ILS courses
in the first year and 21 in the second. The program
required concurrent registration in at least two ILS
courses each semester, and 36 credits had to be completed by the end of the sophomore year. Many of these
were 4-credit courses, which meant that 8 to 12 credits
of the normal 15-credit undergraduate load had to be
reserved for ILS. As requirements changed at the
College level, it became difficult for students to find
room in their schedules for such large blocks of time.
Specifically, the institution of a foreign language
requirement (1964) and a more stringent mathematics requirement in the College of Letters and Science discouraged incoming students from committing themselves
to a two-year program not geared to meeting those
requirements. Mounting prerequisites for most majors,
pressures for early declaration of a major, and above
all, an increasing emphasis throughout the College on
specialization and professionalism, combined to erode
enrollments in the program.

Politics

Finally, the social turmoil of the early seventies
--in competition with the demands for even greater professional training on the campus--brought a variety of
pressures to bear on ILS that were impossible to
balance. Job-conscious undergraduates gravitated away
from the program toward departments whose offerings fit
their prospective careers, while activists, drawn to
the program by its image of "alternative education,"
balked at its historical organization, expecting more
"socially relevant" courses. Again, as in the Meiklejohn years, political tempers flared. Residents
murmured darkly about "out-of-state troublemakers."
Faculty drifted away, some bitter. In these years
there were frequent debates about curricular reform,
but no clear consensus emerged. While it is true that
by 1979 many of these special stresses had been eased,
the chronic problems remained unsolved. The faculty
had lost much of its original unity of purpose, and so
had the students. Fine teaching and dedicated leadership were not enough to stem continued enrollment
losses and administration ire.

The New Integrated Liberal Studies Program: Reforms

These were the issues confronting us as we met to restructure the program in the fall of 1980. Certainly the problems were daunting, but we had the advantage of starting fresh, an immediate crisis to motivate us, and the assurance that we could not possibly make matters worse. The publicity surrounding the near-demise of the program had been a spur to faculty recruitment; that much we recognized from our own response. Other potential volunteers were identified by word of mouth. We sought colleagues who had demonstrated a genuine enthusiasm for undergraduate teaching as well as a cast of mind congenial to interdisciplinary thought. It was our policy to approach only tenured faculty from the disciplines to avoid any repetition of past controversies over non-tenure track appointments. We also wanted to prevent junior faculty from joining at possible damage to their positions in the home departments during their probationary years. The results of this recruiting campaign were more successful than we had expected.

Personnel

Of the continuing faculty, Herbert Howe and Barry Powell, both classicists, had team-taught a course in Greek and Roman culture, combining history, literature, and art. Another colleague, Gretchen Schoff, taught a popular theme course called "The Interpretation of Technology in Literature," which we wanted to retain. With this link to the past, precedent was set for two kinds of interdisciplinary courses in the new curriculum: historical sequences in the mode of history of ideas, and what later we decided to call contemporary topics courses to build upon and follow them.

When, early on, Daniel Siegel and David Lindberg, two historians of science, joined the planning group, the concept of historical sequences received additional support. In this sense, personnel was destiny.

We soon agreed that our primary aim would be to offer an inducement to students to satisfy a good portion of their breadth requirements from ILS courses, but we lacked representatives from the natural and physical sciences and also from the social sciences. We therefore went on to recruit in these areas, now with a better idea of what was needed. Robert March (Physics), Timothy Allen (Botany), and Charles Anderson (Political Science) joined, followed later by Robert

Sack (Geography) and Joseph Elder (Sociology). Thus, over the year, the planning committee expanded, and in weekly meetings we discussed course proposals with one another and set priorities for the curriculum. John Lyons (English) and Haskell Fain (Philosophy) also participated. At one time or another, fourteen faculty were involved.

Educational Philosophy

In retrospect, it seems unusual that we spent so little time discussing educational philosophy, but we proceeded on the assumption that practical solutions were needed for immediate problems. As Dr. Johnson once remarked: "Depend upon it, sir, when a man knows he is to be hanged in a fortnight, it concentrates his mind wonderfully." Indeed, there was remarkable unanimity in our thinking. We all seemed comfortable with the goals of the former program, which were to counter the fragmentation of undergraduate education and to provide a common ground of learning. We now considered how best to achieve these goals. We concluded that busy students in the '80s might well be attracted to a "package" of integrated courses as an alternative to the wide array of unrelated electives scattered across the College Catalog.

The one question that we discussed at length was what we meant by "integration." Consistently, answers were framed in terms of what we felt we could teach best. We determined, first, that integration would be provided both within the separate courses by means of their interdisciplinary focus--resulting, perhaps in some unfortunately long course titles--and, second that integration would be provided within the program as a whole by connecting the courses through a pattern of related sequences. These were the guidelines to which we referred whenever questions arose regarding the suitability of any course. The entire faculty, it should be noted, discussed in detail the syllabus of each new course proposed. As Robert March has remarked: "this process was in itself an intellectually broadening and stimulating experience." At least that was true for those of us who boarded early; later shipmates found a crew to greet them--and had the benefit of a corresponding increase in constructive comments.

During this period we produced only a scant paragraph of dogma: "As in the past, ILS accepts its mission to integrate undergraduate education by emphasizing interdisciplinary courses as valuable in them-

selves and as a necessary background for more specialized work in the student's later years. We affirm the
principles of general education and aim to provide an
overview of important themes, ideas, and developments
in Western civilization. We hope thereby to provide a
sense of continuity for students who will go on to choose
a variety of majors.

Interim Program

But if our proposal appeared modest, we had undertaken a fundamental remodeling of the program. The
two continuing courses were altered so as to fit better
with the new ones; two courses were adapted from other
departments; and eight new courses were developed and
introduced. During 1980-81, freshmen were presented
with an "interim" program consisting of some old and
some transitional courses, while the concept of a
sophomore year was dropped temporarily from the curriculum. Simultaneously the new courses were submitted
for approval to the Executive Committees of the three
Faculty Divisions of the College (Humanities, Physical
Sciences, Social Studies) charged with such review. A
few of these proposals led to negotiations with departments who objected to possible infringement of their
subject matters, but in the end, the courses were
approved. The new curriculum as a whole, along with a
plan to alter radically the structure of the program,
was then presented to the ad hoc Committee on General
Education that had been appointed by the Dean. In
December, 1980, this committee, chaired by Professor
Leonard Berkowitz of the Department of Psychology, en-
dorsed our proposals and so reported to the Dean, who
agreed to extend the program at least through 1983-84.

Structural Revisions

The new curriculum, which came into effect in the
fall of 1981, is geared toward satisfying the breadth
requirements of the College of Letters and Science. A
total of 12 credits is offered in each of the subject
areas (humanities, natural sciences, social studies) as
defined by these requirements. The courses, which are
discussed in greater detail below, are distributed as
follows (H=humanities credit; L=literature credit;
N=natural science credit; S=social studies credit;
P=physical science credit; B=biological science credit):

200:        Critical Thinking and Expression. 3 cr.
            (H) Sem. I.
201-202:   Western Culture: Science, Technology,

	Philosophy. 3-3 cr. (N) Sem. I & II.
203-204:	Western Culture: Literature and the Arts. 3-3 cr. (H) (L) Sem. I & II.
205-206:	Western Culture: Political, Economic, and Social Thought. 3-3 cr. (S) Sem. I & II.
251:	Contemporary Physical Sciences. 3 cr. (P) Sem. I.
252:	Contemporary Life Sciences. 3 cr. (B) Sem. II.
254:	Literature and Contemporary Issues. 3 cr. (H) (L) Sem. II.
255-265:	Contemporary Social Sciences. 3-3 cr. (S) Sem. I & II.

Each course in the program has been reduced uniformly to 3 credits; the requirement of concurrent registration in two or more courses has been dropped; and courses are now open to any student in any year. The thrust of these several structural revisions is to permit flexibility in distributing ILS courses over the full four-year undergraduate program. To further encourage students who begin as freshmen to stay with the program, a certificate now is awarded, with designation noted on the final transcript, to students who complete 21 credits of ILS courses. The certificate attests to the student's accomplishment in completing a program of interdisciplinary study in addition to a major. It is possible that such notation may be of interest to employers or to graduate schools insofar as breadth in a candidate is considered a desired trait.

Requirements as Incentives

Recognizing that today's student is preoccupied with professional goals, we have tried, in other words, to match the benefits of ILS with student interests. It may be that students with well-defined professional goals will avail themselves only of those ILS courses outside their major areas, but it is too early to tell if indeed this will be the pattern. Under this more flexible arrangement, the occasional student can benefit from ILS courses, too, whether or not he or she elects to participate in the full program. Obviously, we hope to increase enrollments by these strategies and to remove the deterrents associated with the previous requirements.

Students

Student response after a year has been encouraging. Total enrollment in ILS courses in the fall semester increased from 487 in 1980 to 580 in 1981, and there were even waiting lists in some courses. Registration in the spring semester of 1981 was even more dramatic. In 1980-81, only 247 continued in the second semester; in 1981-82, there were 470. Of course, it is difficult to compare these figures to past years when all ILS students were enrolled in several courses concurrently. (In 1980, 192 students accounted for the total registration of 487 throughout the various courses). But more sophomores and upperclassmen now appear on our registration lists, and that is a cause for optimism.

Who are the new ILS students? It would be difficult to characterize them. Most are Wisconsin residents. Some are extremely enthusiastic, but although our freshmen seem more curious and more highly motivated than their peers, as a group they do not appear to be necessarily more able or better prepared. The upperclassmen are diverse. A small number from the University's new Medical Scholars program is enrolled, but these have not made their presence noticeable as did the Ford Foundation scholars in the 1950s, who contributed to the image of ILS as an elite, competitive enclave. We do not wish to revive that reputation. Student-faculty relations so far have been excellent.

Faculty

Regarding faculty, ILS now has at its core a new group of volunteers who have a stake in the program that they have initiated. Camraderie at present is strong. We all feel the benefits of interacting with colleagues from other disciplines, and all would say that the challenge of designing a curriculum has been stimulating. But history suggests that no structure can rely indefinitely on enthusiasm. To address this concern, we have asked the administration to find means of crediting ILS workload to the home department of each instructor. In this way, faculty will continue to contribute to the workload of their departments, and they will receive credit for the students that they teach. Inasmuch as this will increase the credit-hour base of the departments, those departments may be more willing in the future to allow their faculty to teach in ILS. We believe that such an arrangement--which in a sense pays interest to the departments from which faculty are borrowed--is important to the long-range health of an interdisciplinary program in a university organized along disciplinary lines. For voting purposes, all "loaned" faculty actually teaching in the ILS program, or who have taught in it within the preceding two academic years, are members of the ILS Executive Committee. All lecturers in ILS are tenured in their home departments. Those departments currently represented on the ILS faculty include: Classics, English, General Engineering, History of Science, Physics, Botany, Political Science, Geography, Sociology and Philosophy.

Curriculum

The new curriculum, reflecting this diversity, offers a set of introductory courses that are organized historically, tracing the achievements of Western civilization from antiquity to the modern period. Taken concurrently, ILS 201-206 provide a synoptic view of literature and the arts; science, technology, and philosophy; and political, economic and social thought. Wherever possible, the syllabi for these courses have been synchronized, so that students may be able to make connections on a weekly basis. The remaining courses in the natural sciences, social studies, and the humanities cover contemporary topics. By contrast, these courses are more loosely orchestrated, and some are arranged thematically. In the sciences, one course is physical and the other biological, as required by the College's breadth requirements. Rounding out the curriculum is a communications skills course that serves the entire program. A brief description of each course follows:

ILS 200   Critical Thinking and Expression

The three modes of argument and expression: verbal, visual, numerical. Critical thinking about how these modes are structured and used. Practice in, and interpretation of, the three modes. Gretchen Schoff (General Engineering) and others.

ILS 201   Western Culture: Science, Technology, Philosophy I.

Western science and technology in the making. Major developments, viewed in their philosophical and social context, from antiquity to the 17th century. David Lindberg (History of Science).

ILS 202   Western Culture: Science, Technology, Philosophy II.

Introduction to selected basic themes in modern physical and biological science in historical context (late 17th to early 20th centuries); interactions with technology, philosophy and society. Daniel Siegel (History of Science).

ILS 203   Western Culture: Literature and the Arts I.

The development of literature and the arts in the ancient and medieval world: Akhnaton's Egypt, Homer's Troy, Euripides' Athens, Virgil's Rome, Dante's Florence. Literature and art in the context of society and ideas. Barry Powell (Classics).

ILS 204   Western Culture: Literature and the Arts II.

The development of literature and the arts from the Renaissance to the modern period, such figures as Shakespeare and Michelangelo through T.S. Eliot and Picasso. Literature and art in the context of society and ideas. Michael Hinden (English).

ILS 205   Western Culture: Political, Economic and Social Thought I.

The development of Western political, economic and social thought, from its origins in classic Greece and the Judaeo-Christian tradition, through Rome and the Medieval period, to the Renaissance and Reformation. Charles Anderson (Political Science).

ILS 206   Western Culture: Political, Economic and Social Thought II.

The development of Western political, economic and social thought from the Reformation to the present day: the origins, logic and evolution of liberalism, Marxism and organic conservatism as the principal systems of thought of the modern age. Charles Anderson.

ILS 251   Contemporary Physical Sciences.

Twentieth century physical theory and its applications in the physical sciences and technology. Relativity and the quantum theory; modern cosmology and astrophysics; the quantum basis of chemistry and molecular biology; nuclear physics and nuclear power technology; quarks and gluons; some philosophical problems connected with these theories. Robert March (Physics).

ILS 252 Contemporary Life Sciences

A systems-oriented approach to the interrelation of plants and humans in their evolution and cultural development; an historical geographic perspective concluding with a consideration of eco-systems in 20th century America. Timothy Allen (Botany).

ILS 254 Literature and Contemporary Issues. Topic: The Interpretation of Technology in Literature.

Examination of the world of modern science and technology as the literary artist sees it. Study of writers who have confronted and interpreted the implications of new creations: the computer, the spaceship, nuclear power, biological manipulation. Gretchen Schoff.

ILS 255 Contemporary Social Sciences I: The Analysis of Social Issues

The critical use of systematic methods of social, political, economic, and ethical inquiry in analyzing social issues and in making deliberate and informed judgments about them. Joseph Elder (Sociology); Haskell Fain (Philosophy).

ILS 256 Contemporary Social Sciences II: Theories and Methods.

Introduction to the scope of human behavior and perspectives and modes of analysis employed by contemporary social science including anthropology, economics, human geography, history, political science, psychology, and sociology. Robert Sack (Geography).

A visualization of the curriculum with reference to the breadth requirements, as drawn by Professor Siegel, is given in Table 2.

TABLE 2

Integrated Liberal Studies (ILS) Program
University of Wisconsin, Madison, 1981-82

	Natural Sciences (12 cr.)	Humanities (12 cr.)	Social Studies (12 cr.)
Foundation Course		200 Critical Thinking & Expression	
Historical Sequences	201 Western Culture: Science, Technology, Philosophy I	203 Western Culture: Literature and the Arts I	205 Western Culture: Political, Economic, and Social Thought I
	202 Western Culture: Science, Technology, Philosophy II	204 Western Culture: Literature and the Arts II	206 Western Culture: Political, Economic and Social Thought II
Contemporary Sequences	251 Contemporary Physical Sciences		255 Contemporary Social Sciences I
	252 Contemporary Life Sciences	254 Literature and Contemporary Issues	256 Contemporary Social Sciences II

A casual comparison of this curriculum to the original ILS curriculum of 1948 might lead to the conclusion that the former curriculum served as a model. It is interesting that no reference was made to the old curriculum during our planning process, and we were surprised to discover the parallels later. Of course, if one is to assume an historical model for an integrated curriculum, certain developments are likely to follow. Moreover, it may be that the historical model is the approach best suited to the Madison campus, where faculty are compartmentalized by research units, many of which are organized along historical lines.

Another aspect of the curriculum worth noticing is its apparent emphasis on science. In fact, science is featured no more prominently than the humanities or social studies, but it certainly is given equal weight. Indeed, one strength of the new program is that the courses integrating science with the other disciplines are actually taught by faculty with science backgrounds. For this reason, we have been permitted to offer these courses for science credit. This service should prove particularly attractive to students majoring in the liberal arts or social studies. So far, enrollments in the literature courses still exceed those in the science courses--but we do expect increases in these areas.

Course in Critical Thinking

One particular innovation in the new curriculum is the "Critical Thinking and Expression" course. Geared to the entering freshman, it stresses analytical and interpretative skills and offers practice in written and oral communication. This is now the only team-taught course in the program, and it is probably the most experimental. The course meets once a week for lecture and twice for workshop exercises in small sections. In the fall of 1981, seven faculty participated, each lecturing in blocks of approximately two weeks. Topics included the use of rhetorical techniques in composition, some principles of logic, characteristics of propaganda, manipulation of statistics and the approach to literature and art as "meaning systems." The objective of the course is to stimulate the students' analytical powers and to provide an introduction to the array of subjects that are treated at greater length elsewhere in the program. Overall, student response, as measured by written evaluations, has been favorable.

Format

In teaching format, the other courses in the program do not differ from standard practice in the university. The normal pattern of two lectures, one discussion, is adhered to (except in courses where there are labs), and grading policies are traditional. Some classes are small, but some are quite large (for example, in 1981-82, the first semester of "Literature and the Arts" enrolled 200). It would be fair to say that, in comparison with former years, the emphasis in ILS now lies more in integrating subject matter than in promoting an alternative educational environment. Certain options in that area have been foreclosed by local history.

Nevertheless, members of the faculty have commented that the "feel of an integrated program is pleasureably different from that of a regular department, and we are aware of the desirability of maintaining close student-faculty contact, as was the case in former years. We suspect that this will become more difficult to achieve as enrollments increase (if they do) and as students spread their coursework over four years instead of registering concurrently, as they used to, for three or four courses at a time. However, we hope to create a core of dedicated students by means of our certificate, offered to those who complete 21 credits by graduation. Presently we are discussing other methods of increasing cohesiveness and continuity in the program. It is still too early to predict what consequences our revisions will have in this area.

The Future

Ahead of us lie related difficulties (assuming that we are extended after 1984). For many years ILS enjoyed the services of an advisor who recruited students during the University's summer orientation program and who continued to counsel those students throughout their undergraduate careers. The current advisor, Dr. Evelyn Howe, retires at the end of the 1981-82 academic year, along with her husband, Professor Herbert Howe. Both will be missed. Moreover, for budgetary reasons, the advisor's position will not be renewed. This loss will impose an added burden on faculty time (which already is strained between ILS and the individual's home department) in the area of advising. And because in the past the advisor also acted as a liaison between faculty and students, the loss will further add to the problem of maintaining contact and cohesiveness.

These issues are of particular concern in light of the extraordinary letters that we have received during the past year from graduates of the ILS program and even from alumni of the Experimental College, who learned of difficulties in the program from alumni newsletters. Their testimony is an inspiring reminder of the benefits to be derived from a truly integrated curriculum. But they stress, too, the close-knit "personality" of the programs they remember and their sense of having participated in a total educational experience quite different from that available elsewhere on the campus. We wonder whether it will be possible to instill comparable memories and eventual loyalties in the students of today.

As we look ahead, other areas of concern include increasing the rewards to faculty who donate their time; providing for replacements when faculty go on leave; generating publicity concerning changes in the program; and of course, ensuring quality instruction, by which we must be judged. Indeed, over the long run it may be more difficult to maintain the program than it was to create it; twice before, that has proved to be the case.

Yet in each instance, faculty at the University of Wisconsin, Madison have renewed their dedication to the principle of general education. In the future, it may become necessary for others to do so once again. In the 1980s it falls to the current group of ILS faculty to build a program suitable to the times. In our efforts we seem to have adopted, almost without realizing it, Meiklejohn's essential goal: "Our primary task is to see, and to help students to see, subjects in their relations."[5] But the structure that is evolving here will not resemble greatly the former ILS program that many alumni recall. Of course, we owe a great debt to the past. As we continue to build and experiment, we increasingly grow to appreciate the idealism and the tenacity of our predecessors.

> Michael Hinden
> Integrated Liberal Studies
> Program

Footnotes

[1] Alexander Meiklejohn, *The Experimental College* (New York: Arno Press, 1971), p. 15.

[2] *Ibid.*, p. 40.

[3] *Ibid.*, p. 106.

[4] Much of the information concerning the early history of ILS has been drawn from Samuel Kellams, *ILS: An Analysis of a General Education Program at the University of Wisconsin* (Ph.D. dissertation, Educational Policy Studies, University of Wisconsin, 1971).

[5] Meiklejohn, p. 164.

HUMANITIES ON THE BORDER: A SPECIAL
INTERDISCIPLINARY PROGRAM FOR A UNIQUE LOCALE
UNIVERSITY OF TEXAS, EL PASO

Neither the raison d'etre nor the conceptual framework within which the Interdisciplinary Humanities Program in Border Studies at The University of Texas at El Paso developed are intelligible without some consideration of the history of The University, its location on the United States-Mexico border, and the formation of the Cross-Cultural Southwest Ethnic Study Center at this University.

The University was founded in 1913 as the State School of Mines on what is now the Fort Bliss Military Reservation. After a seriously destructive fire, the school moved in 1916 to the present campus in the foothills of the Franklin Mountains overlooking the Rio Grande and Juárez, Mexico, on the other side of the river.

Among the important dates in the University's history are the following: in 1919 the school became a branch of the University of Texas System as the Texas College of Mines and Metallurgy; in 1927 the first liberal arts classes were added to the curriculum; in 1949 the name was changed to Texas Western College (enrollment 2,283); and in 1967 the name became The University of Texas at El Paso (enrollment 9,029).

At the present time there are over 15,000 students enrolled in six colleges: Business Administration, Education, Engineering, Liberal Arts, Nursing, and Science, with both baccalaureate and masters degrees offered in all of the colleges; since 1974 the doctorate has been offered in Geological Sciences.

In each of these there have been various consequences of the border location. For one thing, The University of Texas at El Paso has the largest enrollment of Mexican citizens of any college or university in the United States (plus a very large number of Spanish-speaking students from Central and South American nations); for another, there are regular courses taught in Spanish in most academic departments. (In fact, there is a special unit called the Inter-American Science and Humanities Program in which all of the regular courses are taught at first in Spanish while the students take special classes in English as a second language. Then gradually they are taught more and more English). In addition to this, the College of Education at U.T. El Paso has a strong division of bilingual education and the University, as a whole, has a large percentage of Spanish-speaking Chicano students.

Further, there are academic programs of Inter-American Studies and Chicano Studies along with classes on matters concerning Mexico already offered in all of the departments of the College of Liberal Arts; and in these departments and many of these course offerings, topic relating to the U.S.-Mexico borderlands are examined.

Being on the borders of two distinct nations with a great deal of interaction (economic, social, familial, educational, cultural, and other) raises some special problems but also some exciting, challenging possibilities, because, if geography is a fundamental condition for a border, it does not constitute its essence. Of all the borders, the psychological border is the one that we create, utilize, suffer, and enjoy.

Now, if our national border does, to some extent, psychologically separate us, other forces such as conflicting, or at least different, political, economic, social, educational, cultural, and linguistic customs, traditions, and practices are also involved in our contrast.

On the other hand, our mutual border in many ways draws us together--often linking citizens of these two cities/two nations economically, politically, culturally, and personally. The United States-Mexico border can, then, be seen as a limit that limits, as a boundary, that binds, as a protection, as a defense, as a barrier; but our border can also signify dialogue, communication, interchange of ideals and aspirations, and a healthy "living-with" a neighbor marked by mutual respect. Our border separates us and joins us; it can alienate us or foster harmony; it can exaggerate our differences or enhance our similarities; it can promote competition and/or stimulate cooperation.

A goal of the Interdisciplinary Humanities Program in Border Studies has been to accentuate all of the positive elements in the above. Further, there is clearly not one culture on the U.S. side of the border in El Paso, but many: Mexican-American, Tigua Indian, Black, Chinese, and diverse Anglo cultures. The "melting pot" has failed to melt away (though it has at times modified) the cultural diversity of El Paso.

86

Concerning the Mexican side of the border in Cd. Juárez, the statement of Andres Molina Enriques would seem to suffice: "[A] surprising heterogeneity manifests itself in all facets of Mexican life, economics, culture, race, and others, in such a manner that to govern Mexico is like governing different peoples at different stages of history."

In attempting to characterize the diverse cultures of El Paso and Cd. Juárez, great care must be taken to avoid oversimplification.

Thus another task of the Interdisciplinary Humanities Program in Border Studies at U.T. El Paso is to throw some light upon the complex, multicultural situation in our area because it seems essential that policies (economic, political, social and educational) be developed that are based upon an awareness and an understanding of our genuine similarities and differences. Otherwise little results other than hot, angry, destructive denunciations of real or fancied injustices.

The Cross-Cultural Southwest Ethnic Study Center

In September, 1971, the Cross-Cultural Southwest Ethnic Study Center was established at U.T. El Paso under the direction of Z. Anthony Kruszewski with the financial support of a Spencer Foundation grant. As J. Lawrence McConville explained in the May, 1977 Bulletin of the Center: "It aims at helping to prepare courses and instructional units on the ethnic heritage of the Southwest for inclusion in regional Liberal Arts curricula. The Center is also coordinating activities aimed at creating a cultural data bank for illuminating various aspects of interethnic relationships. The Center's Research Associates, conducting projects in the Humanities and Social Sciences, represent a broad interdepartmental spectrum from various Departments of the Colleges of Liberal Arts and Education, and from the Center for Inter-American Studies at U.T. El Paso. They utilize a variety of research techniques to collect, analyze, and interpret sociocultural data on ethnic groups."

In preparing new border studies courses (a primary goal of the Interdisciplinary Humanities Program in Border Studies) not only were several innovative new courses developed, but also various relevant elements from diverse old courses were retained and integrated into these new courses.

Among the many specific activities of the Cross-Cultural Southwest Ethnic Study Center that were to contribute to the creation of a propitious intellectual/cultural environment in which these new courses could develop and flourish were: (1) support for a faculty professional development component that (a) financed faculty travel for necessary research and to appropriate conferences, (b) initiated a number of faculty seminars at which scholars from on-campus and off presented talks designed to stimulate discussion on interdisciplinary course developing/teaching methods and regional concerns, and (c) promoted the development of the cooperative courses themselves; (2) acquisition of research resources, including materials for the CCSWESC library and the University library, and films and tapes (both audio and video); and dissemination of reprints and articles on border studies issues; (3) the encouragement of El Paso community relations activities, including mutual support of and from the El Paso Public Library, the Los Pobres Bilingual Theater, the Chamizal National Memorial, the El Paso Council on the Arts and Humanities, the League of United Latin American Citizens, and others; (4) involvement in inter-university functions, including membership in the Association of Borderlands Scholars, activities with the University of Chihuahua in Cd. Chihuahua, and at The University of Chihuahua in Cd. Juárez, both in Mexico (among which were library exchanges and exchanges of faculty lecturers, students, and dramatic groups), visits to the CCSWESC by scholars (from such universities as San Diego State, Trinity, and Texas Tech) seeking assistance in the development of their own border studies courses or programs, and other visits by interested faculty members from as nearby as The University of Arizona, and Arizona State University, and as far away as the State College of Victoria in Australia and the University of British Columbia in Vancouver, B.C., Canada; and (5) publications for the Center including a periodic Bulletin, a newsletter with translated summaries of new items from the Cd. Juárez newspaper, El Fronterizo, and several books including Chicanos and Native Americans: The Territorial Minorities, Eds. Rudolph O. De la Garza, Z. Anthony Kruszewski, and Thomas Arciniega (Englewood Cliffs: Prentice-Hall, 1973), and Studies on Southwestern Spanish, Eds., Donald J. Bowen and Jacob Ornstein (Rowley, Mass.: Newbury House Publishers).

The Center Staff consisted of Z. Anthony Kruszewski, Director, Jacob Ornstein, Consultant on Bilingualism-Biculturalism, J. Lawrence McConville, Research

Associate in the Humanities and Social Sciences, Maria Elisa Vasquez, Administrative Assistant, Rachel Perez, and Cindy del Rosario, supportive services staff.

Interdisciplinary Humanities Program in Border Studies

In the summer of 1974, the Interdisciplinary Humanities Program in Border Studies was established at The University of Texas at El Paso, financed by a three-year grant of $180,000 from the National Endowment for the Humanities, with a University matching grant of $108,765. It was administered by the CCSWESC.

The goal of this program was to develop courses for a curriculum that would foster a deeper understanding in students of the living cultures of the border-lands: Anglo-American, Chicano, Mexican, Black, and diverse Native American or American Indian tribes on both sides of the U.S.-Mexico border. These courses would relate not just to the southwestern states of the United States (Texas, New Mexico, Arizona, and California) but to the border states of northern Mexico (Baja California Norte, Sonora, Chihuahua [especially], Coahuila, Nuevo Leon, and Tamaulipus). Innovative interdisciplinary teaching methods, field experiences, diverse audio-visual materials, community involvement, and guest lecturers have been regular features of the Border Studies courses that were developed.

By the end of the triennium the courses that had been team-developed and implemented under this program were incorporated into the regular instructional program of The University. Members of the Border Studies Faculty Council who were involved in the course development and implementation were from the Departments of Philosophy (2 members), Political Science (3 members), History (2 members), English (2 members), with one member from Modern Languages, Music, Art, and Linguistics.

The courses developed by this faculty include "Violence and Non-violence in the Southwest" (Philosophy), "American Attitudes Toward the Indian, Black, and Chicano: An Historical Perspective" (History); "La Confluencia de la literatura mexicana y chicana" (Spanish); "Music of the Border" (Music); "The U.S.-Mexico Border since 1848" (History); "Value Orientations: Mexican, Chicano, Anglo, as Revealed in the Humanities" (Philosophy/English); and "Southwestern Border Politics" (Political Science).

This program was described succinctly by J. Lawrence McConville with the following:

> The interdisciplinary Humanities Program in Border Studies is an informal area of concentration designed to supplement regular programs of study for those students desiring to strengthen their appreciation and knowledge of the multicultural context of life in the Southwest of the United States and Northern Mexico. Although the courses in the program are taught in regular departments of the College of Liberal Arts, all are interdisciplinary in character and transcend traditional subject matter distinctions. Particular attention is given to value orientations, the dynamics and consequences of cultures in contact, contemporary life in the El Paso-Cd. Juárez metropolitan area, the effect of the international boundary on regional life, and the fostering of a deeper understanding of each of the contributing cultural traditions, their evolution, transformation and synthesis. The program encourages a blending of perspectives from history, literature, philosophy, and the fine arts, as well as qualitative approaches within the social sciences.

Over the years since their inception, the courses developed within this program have attracted an intriguing mix of students. Since some of the courses practically require bilingualism, it is not too surprising that approximately three-quarters of the students have been Spanish-surnamed; but the fact that a quarter of those enrolled in these Border Studies courses have been students of non-Hispanic ancestry indicates that these courses are by no means seen as somehow restricted to Chicanos or other Spanish-speaking students. It seems clear that substantial numbers of Anglo-American students perceive Border studies courses to be useful in aiding them to achieve a comprehension of the rich, complex, multicultural heritage of the border region.

A widely remarked problem with ethnic studies programs at American universities is that they tend to enroll an overwhelmingly large percentage of members of the ethnic group being studied with minute numbers of other students. This problem has been avoided to a large extent at U.T. El Paso. As McConville puts it, "While comparative data is lacking at this time, there is probably no other ethnic-related curriculum at any other institution of higher learning which has succeeded in attracting such large numbers of mainstream Anglo-

Americans."

It is also significant to note that over 80% of the students enrolled in these Border Studies courses majored in a department other than the department in which the course was taught, which indicates that these courses have had considerable appeal to students who simply want to supplement their major with a regional-istic/humanistic focus.

The Border Studies Faculty Council had frequent meetings during the course development period at which concepts of "borders," of "interdisciplinary courses and programs," and of "humanities" were discussed at length. At these meetings there were also reports presented by the various committees developing the courses, during which objections and suggestions were shared.

Among the important intellectually and culturally enriching projects of the Interdisciplinary Humanities Program in Border Studies were a series of conferences at which scholars from U.T. El Paso and other univer-sities would share information, insights, and conclu-sions. Among these conferences was one titled "Humani-ties on the Border" (May, 1976), with specialists from U.T. El Paso, the University of Santa Clara, the Uni-versity of Chihuahua, the University of Utah, New Mexico State University, Sul Ross State University, Laney College, The University of Chicago, Texas A. & I. University, El Paso Community College, The University of Arizona, and San Antonio College, plus the author, Rodolfo Anaya, and the sculptor, Luis Jimenez (neither of whom were connected with a university) participating. Topics covered included value orientations on the border, borderlands literature, the border and the Mexican Revolution, and cross-cultural influences of arts in border areas.

There was, the following year (May, 1977), another conference titled, "Border Studies: Recent Developments and Future Trends," which included panel discussions on border studies in Political Science, Sociology, Anthro-pology, Economics, Geography, History, Drama, Philoso-phy, Literature, and Folklore. Most of the participants were from The University of Texas at El Paso faculty, but there were important guest speakers from Colorado College, the University of Texas at Austin, the Univer-sity of California at San Diego, and the University of Texas at San Antonio.

Later there were mini-conferences on border linguistics, on the borderlands and the Third World, on the contemporary ethnology of the borderlands, and on language and society in the borderlands, each of which involved faculty and students from The University, faculty from other universities, and speakers from the local El Paso community.

Each of these activities were extremely useful for the faculty members who were developing or who had developed the innovative, interdisciplinary courses and were teaching them.

Now it may be of interest to examine the course that the author of this paper has been teaching for the last several years to give a specific example of what has been done. It is a relatively typical instance of course development and implementation in this program.

A Course: Violence and Non-Violence in the Southwest

A team of faculty members from the Departments of Philosophy, History, and Political Science, plus J. Lawrence McConville, met for several months exploring concepts and themes relating first to the topics of violence and non-violence in general, and then to these same topics in relation to the past and present situation in the Southwestern portion of the United States-- especially as regards Chicanos and American Indians in this area.

In the course that we developed, after an examination of basic concepts and the terminology to be employed in our examination of types of violence and their relationships, questions were examined concerning whether violence is innate or acquired, and if acquired, what are the causes. Next cultural, political, religious, and philosophical alternatives to violence were considered, after which the causes and character of Chicano violence were analyzed; then educational, social, political, economic, and cultural alternatives to Chicano violence were studied. Finally, historical, political, economic, and educational factors relating to Native American violence were presented, followed by a consideration of anthropological, educational, cultural, and religious elements in American Indian life that are opposed to violent behavior.

Over the several years that this class has been taught (in every Spring and First Summer academic session) a substantial number of guest speakers have contributed to its success. These include two anthropologists, three political science professors, teachers of Spanish, education, linguistics, and history, three philosophers, Chicano poets, dramatists, dancers, social workers, and militants from the El Paso community, an Anglo peace activist, and two Anglo psychologists, also from the community, a leader of the Tigua Indian tribe and a Mescalero Apache teacher, and, finally, a Quaker peace leader and a physician-political activists both from Mexico. In the average semester there are eight to ten guest lecturers from various academic disciplines and from diverse ethnic groups.

This course can be termed interdisciplinary, then, in that it was conceived, planned, and developed by a group of faculty members from several academic disciplines; and though it has been "taught" (in a very special sense) by one professor, the contributions of a wide variety of guest speakers and the utilization of topics and materials from diverse fields do give it such a character. (It might be noted that this seems natural, even inevitable, considering the subject matters examined.)

The class has also viewed a number of films over the years, including six on violence and non-violence, six on American Indians, and four on Chicanos, plus audio tapes of Cesar Chavez and Martin Luther King, Jr., and a large number of recordings of music of war and peace (by persons like Joan Baez, Bob Dylan, Theodore Bikel and Tom Lehrer). The students have performed plays like Daniel Berrigan's Trial of the Catonsville Nine, Luis Valdez' Los Dos Caras del Patroncito, and a play titled Cool Dawn's Story (adapted by John Haddox from an episode in Thomas Klise's novel The Last Western).

Every semester the class plays certain American Indian games like the Pawnee Indian "handgame" and the "Patol Stick game" at a feast with Indian songs, dances, art, and food.

In addition, every time the class has been offered, the students (at least some of them) and the professor have gone on a field trip. These trips have included ones to the Navajo Community College in Tsaile, Arizona, to the Academia de la Nueva Raza in Dixon, New Mexico, to the University of Chihuahua in Ciudad Chihuahua, Mexico, to the Mescalero Apache reservation (several times), and to the Indian World's Fair at Firebird Lake, Arizona.

The grades for the students are based on a journal which they are required to keep each class, including a summary of what went on each time and their personal response to it, two research papers concerning a selected list of peace leaders or peace organizations (with a report on an interview with a local figure as a possible option in place of one of the research papers), and a "creative work" which is shared with the entire class at the end of the semester. The creative work is the product of the student's imagination (as applied to the topics treated in the class) expressed in a song or dance or painting or drawing or sculpture, or any one of countless creative media. (This emphasis on the imaginative/creative dimension of human activity is based upon a realization of the need for education generally, and this course in particular, to challenge students to come up with new and original approaches to traditional problems--and to have their affective faculties--their feelings--involved.)

The text for the course is <u>The Politics of Non-violent Action</u> by Gene Sharp, but the class members are also given a large number of articles as handouts. The articles are by such philosophers as Albert Camus, Martin Buber, Gabriel Marcel, and Antonio Caso, and by a variety of authors such as Dom Helder Camara, Herberto Sein, Norman Cousins, Daniel Berrigan, Thomas Merton, John Vasconcellos, and James McGuiness.

Conclusion

This interdisciplinary course and the entire Interdisciplinary Humanities Program in Border Studies have been quite popular with students at The University of Texas at El Paso who, in course evaluations, have generally made strongly favorable comments about the regional, multi-dimensional relevance of the courses and the program.

For the faculty members involved, the experience has been, again general, one of genuine personal and academic growth (involving a movement away from narrow departmental isolation and overspecialization). A further benefit for faculty has been the opportunity afforded by this program to form close, cooperative relationships among faculty members of diverse departments. A supportive sharing of ideals, insights, and information has been highly salutary for a university faculty sometimes more prone to competitive, even adversary, relationships.

Further, the faculty (and hopefully the students) involved in this interdisciplinary border studies program have learned that instead merely of a conflict of cultures, there is also a complementary character to the diverse cultures present in our communities. There is an emphasis in these courses on the potential and actual advantages of a multicultural setting, and a prizing of the diversity present. As theologian Harvey Cox has put it, "Let us envision [a society] where our differences delight us and in their depths we find a common humanity"--surely a fitting motto for this interdisciplinary program.

Finally, for The University of Texas at El Paso, these courses developed in this program remain alive and strong. They will, it is hoped, be part of a foundation upon which this university can build academic programs that will make it a major contributor to a vital, informed spirit of interethnic and international understanding and cooperation in the difficult years ahead.*

John H. Haddox
Department of Philosophy

*SCHEDULE--Typical course schedule for Violence and Non-violence in the Southwest.

PHILOSOPHY 3310--VIOLENCE AND NON-VIOLENCE
IN THE SOUTHWEST

SCHEDULE

JAN 20: Introduction and Course Description
(Plan field trip and discuss assignments)

Make distinctions concerning terminology:
Power, force, violence, aggression, revolution,
rebellion.

Discuss questions: Is violence innate or acquired, or partially both? Can generalizations
be made about violence or is each case unique?
Is violence in itself moral, immoral, or mor-
ally neutral?

JAN 25: Types of Violence and Their Relationships

Overt, covert, physical, psychological, personal, impersonal, legal, criminal, individual,
collective, institutional, racial, political,
intraethnic, interethnic, military, economic,
defensive, offensive, justified, unjustified,
conformist, nonconformist.

Ethnic inter-relationships: Assimilation,
acculturation, biculturism, transculturism.

Sources: Violence, J.J.D. Giacomo; Collective
Violence, eds., Short and Wolfgang; The Face
of Violence, J. Bronowski; A Sign for Cain, F.
Wertham.

(Please read handouts to discuss on Thursday.)

JAN 27: Violence: Innate or Acquired?

Discussion of whether violence is natural, in-
stinctive, innate or whether it is learned by
experience (or both).

Sources: African Genesis and The Territorial
Imperative, both by Robert Ardrev; On Aggres-
sion, K. Lorenz; Man and Agression, ed. by
M.F.A. Montague; Man's Aggression, G. Rochlin;
In Defence of Homo Sapiens, J. M. Cook.

96

FEB 1:   Causes of Violence

Discussion of sources of violence: Political, economic, educational, social, psychological, philosophical.

Sources: Why Men Rebel, Ted Gurr; The Rebel, A. Camus; Violence in Modern Literature, ed. J.J. Iorio; Violence and Social Change, H. Bienen; Abolition of Man, C.S. Lewis; On Understanding Violence Philosophically, J.G. Gray; Faith and Violence, T. Merton.

FEB 3:   Violence: Frustration and Anger as Causes

Half-hour of role-playing. Hour-long lecture by psychologist, Edie Eger.

Sources: Education and Ecstacy, Geo. Leonard; Power and Innocence, R. May; The Wretched of the Earth, F. Fanon; Decent and Indecent, B. Spock; Aggression and Altruism, H. Kaufmann; The Anatomy of Human Destructiveness, Erich Fromm.

FEB 8:   Violence: As American as Cherry Pie?

Half-hour of question-raising concerning violence in the United States. Hour-long lecture by Prof. Ed. Leonard of the Political Science Department.

Sources: Without Marx or Jesus, J.F. Revel; "The Great American Frustration," A Macleish; History of Violence in America, Graham and Gurr; American Racism, Daniels and Kitano; Violence and Social Change, E. Bienen; "Power and Coercion," Ed Leonard; Dissent, Power, and Confrontation, ed. A. Klein; Our Violent Past, I.J. Sloan; Violence in America, Thos. Rose; And Keep Your Powder Dry, M. Mead; Our Violent Society, D. Abrahamsen; American Violence, R.M. Brown; America the Violent, O. Demaris.

(Please read on alternatives to violence in Gene Sharp book for discussion.)

FEB 10: Cultural Alternatives to Violence:

Discussion: cultural values; artistic, literary, dramatic, musical activiites; education for brotherhood and peace.

Sources: "Our Two-Story Culture," Paul Bohannan; Nonviolence in an Aggressive World, A.J. Muste; Neither Victims, Nor Executioners, Albert Camus; Education and Ecstasy, Geo. Leonard; Celebration of Awareness, I. Illich.

(Please prepare a paper on one of the following peace leaders or on a peace organization for presentation to the class on February 24.

Peace leaders to research: César Chávez, Dom Helder Câmara, Jane Adams, Joan Baez, David Harris, Frederick Douglass, Daniel Ellsberg, Mahatma Gandhi, Dag Hammarskjold, Jesus Christ, Francis of Assisi, Martin Luther King, Jr., A. J. Muste, Dorothy Day, Peter Maurin, Linus Pauling, William Penn, Bertrand Russell, Albert Schweitzer, Benjamin Spock, Henry David Thoreau, Sojourner Truth, Mark Twain, Phillip Berrigan, Daniel Berrigan, Ralph Bunche, Daniel Dolci, Ivan Illich.

Peace Organizations to research: American Friends Service Committee, Jane Adams Peace Foundation, Amnesty International, U.C. Committee for UNICEF, Peace Corps, War Resistor's League, Institute for World Order.

FEB 15: Political Alternatives to Violence:

Discussion: Philosophy of Satyagraha; non-violent active resistance (including protest, persuasion, debate, picketing, parading, symbolic public acts, drama, art, music, walkouts, silence, boycotts of products and activities, strikes, withdrawal from the social system involved, fasting, hunger strikes, sit-ins, stand-ins, etc.); achievements of justice; solutions to problems in socio-economic sphere.

Sources: Alternatives to Violence, ed. Larry Ng; The Politics of Non-violent Action, Gene Sharp; Exploring Nonviolent Action, G. Lakey; Exploring Nonviolent Alternatives, G. Sharp; Protest: Pacifism and Politics, James Finn; Conquest of Violence, J. Bondurant; Nonviolence in America, ed. Lynd; The Law of Love, My Non-Violence, Satyagahas, and Nonviolent Resistance, all by M.K. Gandhi; Gandhis Truth, E.

Erikson; The Power of Nonviolence, Gregg; Instead of Violence, A. and L. Weinberg; Non-Violent Action, How it Works, Geo. Lakey; Violence of Aggressive Nonviolent Resistance, P.P. Mouton; Liberation, Revolution, and Freedom, ed. T.M. McFaddon.

FEB 17: Religious and Philosophical Alternatives to Violence I:

Talk on religious and philosophical dimensions of non-violence by Prof. David Hall of the Philosophy Department.

Sources: The Religions of the Oppressed, V. Lanternari; The Non-Violent Cross, James Douglass; They Call Us Dead Men, by Daniel Berrigan; No More Strangers, A Punishment for Peace, and Widen the Prison Gates, all by Philip Berrigan; Peace and Non-Violence, ed., Ed Guinan.

FEB 22: Religious and Philosophical Alternatives to Violence II:

After a brief dramatic reading by members of the class from the Trial of The Catonsville Nine by Daniel Berrigan, there will be a discussion of moral values, a love ethic, inter-ethnic harmony and cooperation, peace organizations, family activities; the achievement by persons of self-identity, self-acceptance, self-valuing, self-determination and self-control.

Sources: Conflict: Violence and Nonviolence, J.V. Bondurant; Liberation Ethics, J.M. Swomley; The Moral Equivalent of War, Wm. James; Christian Pacifism in History, G. Nuttal; An Alternative to War, Gordon Zahn; Which Way to Peace?, B. Russell; Decent and Indecent, B. Spock; Peace on Earth Handbook, L.E. Halvorson.

FEB 24: Student presentation of papers on peace leaders or peace organizations.

(Please read handouts on violent revolutionaries in Latin America.)

MAR 1: Chicano Violence: Possible Inspiration in Mexico (and Elsewhere in Latin America):

Lecture on Villa, Zapata, Flores Magón,
Lombardo Toledano, De Gortari, Guillen,
Guevara, Torres.

Sources: Philosophy of the Urban Guerrilla, A.
Guillen; The Latin American Revolution, D.C.
Hodges; Camilo Torres, G. Guzmán; Camilo
Torres, J.A. Garcia; Che Guevara Speaks, and
Why is the Third World Poor?, both by P. Gheddo;
Conflict and Violence in L.A. Politics, Moreno
and Mitrani; Mexican Marxist, Vicente Lombardo
Toledano, R.P. Million; The Wind That Swept
Mexico, Brenner and Leighton; The U.S. and
Pancho Villa, C.C. Clendenen; The Modern Cul-
ture of L.A., J. Franco; Zapata and the Mexican
Revolution, J. Womack; Memoirs of Pancho Villa,
M.L. Guzman; Yesterday in Mexico, J.W.F. Dulles;
The Guerrillas, J. Larteguy; Sembradores,
Ricardo Flores Magón, J. Gómez-Quiñones; Revo-
lutionaries, Traditionalists and Dictators in
Latin America, H.E. Davis; The Underdogs, M.
Azuela; La Revolución Mexicana, R. Flores
Magón; De Martí a Castro, José Martí and F.
Castro; Retrato de Camilo Torres, H. Bojorge.

MAR 3:   Chicano Violence: Causes and Character:

Lecture by Ernesto Briones of the Department
of Philosophy.

Sources: The Forgotten American, L.F. Hernández;
The Unusual Mexican, R.L. Martínez; The Chicano
Movement, A. Delgado.

MAR 8:   Chicano Violence: Historical Factors:

1. Movie: I am Joaquín.

2. Discussion of historical background led by
   Professor Oscar Martínez of the Department
   of History.

Sources: Somos Chicanos--Strangers in Our Land,
D.F. Gómez; North From Mexico and The Mexicans
in America both by C. McWilliams; The Story of
the Mexican American and Occupied America both
by Rudy Acuña; The Chicanos, Meier and Rivera;
A Documented History of the Mexican American,
ed. W. Moquín; Aztecas del Norte, J.D. Forbes;
Foreigners in Their Native Land, ed. D.J.
Weber; Furia y Muerte, Los Bandidos Chicanos,

100

Castillo and Camarillo; The Mexican American: His Life Across Four Centuries, G.T. Martínez; The Chicanos, Gilberto López y Rivas.

(Please read Ricardo Sánchez' Selections.)

MAR 10: Chicano Violence: Literature

Ricardo Sánchez, Chicano poet, lecture and discussion.

Sources: Chicano, Richard Vásquez; Canto Y Grito Mi Liberación and HechizoSpells both by Ricardo Sánchez; Pocho, J.A. Villareal; The Chicano: From Caricature to Self-Portrait, ed. Ed Simmen; With the Ears of Strangers, C. Robinson; Los Quatro, A.B. Delgato and others; From the Belly of the Shark, ed. Walter Lowenfels; The Chicanos: Mexican American Voices, ed. Ludwig and Sentibañez; The Plumb Pickers, R. Barrios; Floricanto en Aztlan, Alurista; The Gypsy Wagon, ed. A.R. Rodríguez; Regional Dictionary of Chicano Slang, Vásquez and Vásquez; Restless Serpents, Barciaga and Zamora.

(Please prepare a paper for a May 3 presentation to the class on either:)

A. Interview of a person someway involved with violence/nonviolence war/peace issues (military recruiter, war veteran, law enforcement officer, contact sports coach, clergyman, member active with peace organization)

B. Local Research
    Visit grammar school and talk with children re violence, peace, conflict, etc.; violence and media (El Paso Anglo, Chicano Juárez Mexicana); study of stereotypes (Indians and Chicanos in Ysleta); Compare teachings of "Mexican War"--1846-1848 period in El Paso and Juárez; Mexican/Chicano relations on campus; etc.

MAR 15: Chicano Violence--General Discussion of Historical, Literary, Socio-economic and Political Factors.

Sources: Los Chicanos, an Awakening People,

J.H. Haddox; El Espejo and Voices, both by O.
Romano-V.; Pensamientos on Los Chicanos, Elin
Carranza; La Causa Chicana, M.M. Mangold; We
Are Chicanos, ed. P. Ortega; Pain and Promise,
ed. Ed Simman; Aztlen, Steiner and Váldes;
La Raza: The Mexican Americans, S. Steiner;
Tijerina and The Courthouse Raid, Julian Samora;
The Political Socialization of the Mexican
American People, R.C. Guzmán; El Político, J.A.
Gutierrez; Tijerina: Land Grant Conflict in New
Mexico, J. Jenkinson; Shootout at Tierra
Amarilla, R. Salas; Chicano Politics Readings,
F.L. García; Grito: Reyes Tijerina and the New
Mexico Land Grant War of 1967, R. Gardner.

(Please read the handouts on non-violent
revolutionaries in Latin America.)

MAR 17: Alternatives to Chicano Violence: Mexican and
other Latin American NonViolent Revolutionaries: Lecture and discussion.

Sources: The Desert is Fertile, Helder Câmara;
Antonio Caso, Philosopher of Mexico, J.H.
Haddox; The Other Mexico and Alternating Cur-
rent, both by Octavio Paz; Dom Helder Câmara,
J. de Broucker; To Live is to Love and Homage
to the American Indians, both by Ernesto Car-
denal; A New Moral Order, D. Goulet; A Theology
of Liberation, G. Gutierrez; Revolution Through
Peace, H. Camara; Liberation Ethics, J.M.
Swomley, Jr.; Pedagogy of the Oppressed,
Paolo Freire; Octavio Paz, G.G. Wing; History
of the Church in Latin America, E. Dussell;
My Life for my Friends, the Guerrilla Journal
of Nestor Paz, Christian.

MAR 29: Alternatives to Chicano Violence: Educational.

Forty-five minute movie (Tlatelolco) and discussion.

Sources: El Cuaderno (Journal); Mexican Ameri-
cans in School, T.P. Carter; El Plan de Santa
Barbara: Introduction to Chicano Studies,
Duran and Bernard; Mexican Americans: A Hand-
book for Educators, J. Forbes; DeSchooling
Society, I. Illich.

MAR 31: Alternatives to Chicano Violence: Social,
Political, Economic.

102

Tape of talks by César Chávez; movie, Corrido; and discussion.

Sources: Forty Acres: César Chávez and the Farmworkers, Mark Day; Shadows in the Valley, F.A. Kostyu; Delano, J.G. Dunne; La Raza Unida Party in Texas, M. Compean; Sal Si Puedes, Peter Matthiessen; La Causa: the California Grape Strike, Fusco and Horwitz; Huelga: The First Hundred Days of the Great Delano Grape Strike, Eugene Nelson; Chicanos: Social and Psychological Perspectives, Wagner and Hang; Mexican-Americans, an Awakening Minority, M. Servin; Viva la Raza, Julian Nava; Chicano: The Evolution of a People, Rosaldo, Calvert, and Seligman; Mexican Americans in the U.S., C. Bustamante; Emerging Faces: The Mexican Americans, A. Cabrera; The Changing Mexican-American, Rudolph Gomez; La Causa Chicana, ed. M.M. Mangold; César Chávez, Autobiography of La Causa, Jacques Levy.

(Please read articles on José Vasconcelos.)

APR 5:   Alternatives to Chicano Violence: Cultural.

Student presentation of play, Las Dos Caras del Patroncito, movie, Tapestry, and a brief discussion of the philosophy of José Vasconcelos.

Sources: Vasconcelos of Mexico, Philosopher and Prophet, J.H. Haddox; Chicano Literature, A. Castañeda Schular; Background of Mexican American Literature, P.D. Ortega; Bless Me, Ultima, R. Anaya; Antología del Saber Popular; Chicano Poetry Anthology, 1968-1973; The Proud People!, H.J. Alford; Christianity and Culture, V.P. Elizondo; There Are No Flights Out Tonight, Ricardo Teall; Festival de Flor y Canto.

APR 7:   Alternatives to Chicano Violence: Cultural II.

Lectures and discussion of Chicano dance and theatre by Rosa Guerrero and Héctor Serrano.

Sources: Actos, Luis Váldes; Dances of Anahuac, Marti and Kurath; The Mexican American and Dramatic Literature, Héctor Serrano; Chicano Drama, El Grito book series.

103

APR 12: Native American Violence: Causes and Character.

1. Movie, As Long as the Rivers Run.

2. Discussion of movie and questionraising.

Sources: Indians are People, Too, R.M. Brenson; Awakening Minorities, J.R. Howard; Man's Rise to Civilization as shown by the Indians of North America, P. Farb.

APR 14: Native American Violence: Historical Factors.

Movies: American Indian Before and After the White Man Came and discussion.

Sources: The Tortured Americans, Robert Burnette; Of Utmost Good Faith, Vine Deloria; The Death of the Great Spirit, Earl Shorris; Short History of Indians in the U.S., E.H. Spicer; Bury My Heart at Wounded Knee, Robert Burnette and J. Koster; America's Concentration Camps, C. Embry; The American Indian, The First Victim, J. David Ed; The American Heritage Book of Indians, Wm. Brandon; Indians in North America, H. Driver.

(Please read my articles on American Indians for discussion.)

APR 19: Native American Violence: Political and Educational Factors.

Lecture and discussion on the Native American and Political and educational situation.

Sources: Our Brother's Keeper, E.S. Kahn; Custer Died for Your Sins, Road to the Trial of Broken Treaties, We Talk, You Listen, by Vine Deloria; Red Power, The American Indian's Fight for Freedom, A.M. Josephy; Chicanos and Native Americans: The Territorial Minorities, eds., de la Garza, Kruszewski, Arciniega; Indian Oratory, W.C. Vanderwerth; The Indian and the White Man, W. Washburn; Alcatraz is not an Island; Awakening Minorities, J.R. Howard; The Road to Wounded Knee, R. Burnette.

APR 21: Alternatives to Native American Violence: Anthropological Factors.

Student presentation of a play Cool Dawn's Tale; along with a traditional handgame and a discussion.

Sources: The Way, S.H. Hitt and S. Steiner; Tales of the North American Indians, ed. Slith Thompson; The Lost Universe, G. Welthfish; The Navajo, R. Underhill; Culture in Crisis, J. Collier and L. Thompson; Four Ways of Being Human, G. Litsky; The Hopiway, L. Thompson and A. Josephy.

(Please read articles on Indian education for discussion.)

APR 26:   Alternatives to Native American Violence: Educational Factors.

Discussion of BIA schools and culture-based and non-culture-based Indian schools.

Sources: The Search for American Indian Identity, H.Hertzberg; The New Indians, Stan Steiner; Education Across Cultures, Zintz and Ulibarri; To Live on This Earth, E. Fuchs and R.J. Harighurst; The Native American Today.

APR 28:   Alternatives to Native American Violence: Cultural and Religious Factors.

Movie and discussion.

Sources: When the Legends Die, Hal Bourland; The Indian Heritage of America, A.M. Josephy; To Touch the Earth, T.C. McLuhan; American Indian Religions, J.M. Hurdy; Lame Deer, Seeker of Visions, John Lame Deer; Black Elk Speaks, ed. John Neihardt; The Sacred Pipe, ed. J.E. Brown, Ghost Dance Religions, J. Mooney; God is Red, Vine Deloria; Hopi Ethics, R.E. Brandt; The Fourth World of the Hopis, H. Courlander; Red Man's Religion, R. Underhill; Land of the Spotted Eagle, Luther Standing Bear; Soul of the Indian, Chas. Eastmen; The Indian Book, N. Curtis, Burlin, ed.; House Made of Dawn and The Way to Rainy Mountain, both by N. Scott Monaday; American Indian Prose and Poetry, ed. Margot Astrov; The Magic World, ed., Wm. Brandon; The Sky Clears, A. Grove Day; Snaking the Pumpkin, J. Rothenberg; Sun Chief, The

Autobiography of a Hopi, ed. Leon Simmons; The Emergent Native Americans, D.E. Walker, Jr.; Seeing With a Native Eye, ed., W.H. Capps.

MAY 3: Student presentation of research projects assigned on March 10.

MAY 5: Presentation of Creative Work.

(There will be a field trip to Ganado Indian College or the Mescalero Reservation or the Zuni Pueblo or to other locations that might be suggested.)

John H. Haddox
Department of Philosophy

INTEGRATED HUMANITIES PROGRAM
UNIVERSITY OF SOUTH DAKOTA

In 1975, the University of South Dakota began what is best described as an experiment in integrated regional studies sponsored by the College of Arts and Sciences and the National Endowment for the Humanities. We contemplated a two-year program in rural studies, hoping, first, to revitalize the Humanities by combining certain basic requirements into a single sequence of courses and, second, to shift some of the emphasis of course content to social values, ethics and critical thinking.

What follows is a report of the progress and development of the project during the past five years.

The University of South Dakota is a small, state-supported university, located close to the borders of South Dakota, Iowa, Nebraska, and Minnesota from which it draws most of its students. It offers liberal arts, education, business, fine arts, law, medicine, and technical degrees. The enrollment averages roughly 5,000 students.

The student body is homogeneous: mostly rural, middle class, and Caucasian. This similarity of background is an important reason why the program was given a regional focus. To the degree that students share a common culture, the cultural elements of the region seemed to be a natural source for the themes and issues of the program.

The University as a context for this experiment was also an important factor in our decision. It struggles to address the challenges of very limited resources, sometimes compounded by an extremely pragmatic view on the part of the general population of the role of higher education. Students bring very practical vocational goals from high schools which, themselves, reflect the general public attitudes. Students have had little or no exposure to the contributions of the liberal arts and tend to lack imagination in assessing their own goals and potential.

The organization of the University reflects and tends to reinforce these attitudes. Divisions between areas of knowledge are quite rigid and students are encouraged early to decide upon a course of study. Furthermore, until recently, the University made little effort to attract students to the arts and humanities. Each professional school or program has established its requirements without reference to the contributions of a liberal arts education and (beyond a minimum of requirements in English) to other units of the University. The stress on vocationalism has rendered the departments of Philosophy, Classics, and Modern Languages little more than service departments. Communication and English, while maintaining adequate major programs, have fared little better. The teaching of required courses was bound by tradition and, with outstanding exceptions, routine and stagnant.

This situation has produced a sequence of effects. A general decline in humanities enrollments resulted in diminished resources for the departments suffering the declines. When their resources were shifted elsewhere (because of formula budgeting) departments which were no longer competitive were forced to continue with diminished resources, further reducing the appeal of their courses. This, of course, resulted in greater declines in enrollments and yet further reduction in support.

The net effect has been to make decline in the liberal arts structural or systemic. Decline in enrollments or resources contributed to further decline--diminished attractiveness, lowered potential, and further retrenchment. Innovations which seemed to be desperately needed were difficult, both because the resources were further straitened and because the enthusiasm and morale of those who might have instituted changes had waned.

To address at least some of the sources of decline, in 1975, with the support of the National Endowment for the Humanities, the University instituted a pilot program of integrated humanities called "The Cultural Components of Rural America." The intention was to combine material from Art, Classics, Communication, English, History, Modern Languages, and Philosophy with exercises in thinking, writing, and speaking skills into four related courses comprising 36 semester hours. Roughly half of these credits were intended to fulfill the basic requirements in English composition, speech, western civilization, and area requirements in Humanities. The remainder were designed to become a minor in Humanities for bachelor of arts and bachelor of science degrees in the College of Arts and Sciences.

Faculty development and planning began with the

summer session of 1975. Eight members of the faculty representing the departments listed above were selected by the deans of the colleges and the director. All of the faculty were senior members with considerable teaching experience.

Involving the senior faculty has been a constant feature of the Program. We believed that experienced teachers who were well grounded in their disciplines would be able to adapt their knowledge to the demands of the Program without compromising their disciplines. They have proved to be both adaptable and secure, and we have especially benefited from their support during the early stages of implementation.

The planning session was supported by NEH for six weeks. The purpose was to determine "cultural components" and design and organize four sequential courses of nine credit hours each semester for freshman and sophomore students.

Probably the most challenging task was finding working definitions, or at least descriptions, of "rural" and "culture" without reducing the courses to a study of farming. Every discipline has its own view of cultural components: some thought of them as artifacts or products inspired by the region; others as ideas, prejudices and values; still others as patterns of causes and effects. What emerged was a consensus that the best approach should be by means of cultural "areas" such as creative, political, economic, social, and ethical endeavors.

We finally agreed that each general area should act as a source of relatively specific themes or issues upon which the courses were to be organized. Each theme needed to meet two criteria: 1) to have a significant bearing on the lives of those presently living in the region, and 2) to have a development traceable to sources beyond the region or to regional conditions of the past. A major consideration--whether or not a "component" must be relevant only to the region--was to have interesting consequences in the acceptance of the Program by the University as will be shown later.

The list of organizing themes included such aspects of the region as these:

The Heroic Ideal--discoverers, settlers, the development of the West,
Pastoralism, Agrarianism, and the agricultural

revolution,
Ethnic Diversity and the theory of the melting
    pot,
Religious Diversity and the religious community,
Social Unrest and social revolution,
Populism, Progressivism and political conservatism,
Women in the West--fact, fancy, and fiction,
Landscape, the environment, and environmental
    ethnics,
Technology and values.

Each participating department contributed what it could of content, materials, and activities to these themes. The selection was less difficult for Art, Philosophy, and literature whose materials do not always require an historical context. However, it caused some difficulties for history, which seemed to be faced with the development of not one but ten chronologies.

The first model of the courses selected British and American literature, American and European history, and written composition for freshmen in the units covering discovery, agriculture, religious diversity, social unrest, and populism. Art, speech, European literature, ethics, and logic covering ethnic diversity, women, the environment, and technology were reserved for sophomores. The freshmen courses were taught by two members of the Department of English and one from the Department of History. The sophomore courses were taught by one member each from the Departments of Art, Philosophy, Classics, Modern Languages, and Communication.

The texts included single works, anthologies, social histories, and handbooks (for composition and speech). The existing texts were far from perfect for our purposes, although we discovered some very interesting and stimulating materials including Nisbet, The Social Philosophers, Norling, Timeless Problems in History, Conron, The American Landscape, and Dinnerstein, Nichols, & Reimers, Ethnic Groups in the Building of America. Of the individual works, Rolvaag's Giants in the Earth has proved to be essential. Other selections included standard British, American, and European authors and ancient and modern philosophers.

Frequent and increasingly demanding writing assignments were designed to accompany the work of the freshman year; logic, speech, and debate the second. Brief field trips were scheduled to points of interest such as the Hutterite colonies, ethnic communities, and regional cultural centers for museums and art galleries.

The enrollment for the freshman course was set at thirty. Eventually 28 enrolled. They were fairly representative of the general freshman class in ability and academic interests. Most students were very wary of some features of the program, especially of the commitment to 36 semester hours, of receiving one grade for nine hours, and of the perception that they were enrolling in an honors program.

We have never been able to shed this last stigma which has hampered enrollment from the very beginning. Academic advisors seem to view all non-traditional courses as honors, even though the Integrated Humanities Program tried hard to enroll a cross-section of freshmen students. If the experiment was to tell us anything, we needed to find out what kinds of students benefited and what kinds did not.

By almost any standard, the first year was successful. The morale of the students and faculty held up very well in spite of some confusion caused mostly by inadequate coordination among the three teachers. Both students and faculty had to learn to work together in understanding and sharing goals and in setting standards. Deciding on grades was a little more difficult. If teachers hold anything sacred, it is their absolute authority over grades. The issue was resolved when each teacher submitted a grade for each student for his part of the course while agreeing that an average would determine the final grade.

While that solution still applies, it also still raises questions. A low or failing grade in an entire area could be raised to a passing mark by much higher grades in others. If a student fails composition, the argument goes, should he appear to have passed because he received an "A" in history? While such an event is rare, we are still searching for a wholly satisfactory answer.

Attrition between the first and second years was nearly 50%. Fifteen students enrolled for the third and 12 for the fourth semester. Many students had, by the end of their first year, determined on academic majors and professional programs and were eager to start. Other undergraduate schools such as Education, Fine Arts, and Business listed requirements for sophomores which competed with the Humanities Program, and those schools were reluctant to change their sequence of requirements. While electives were available during the junior and senior years, the lists, often presented as "typical semester schedules," intimidated the students, and faculty advisors felt no great obligation to work out alternative schedules. No single feature of university organization presents greater problems for new programs than requirements listed semester by semester in the general catalogue.

Evaluations at the end of the first and second years showed a high level of satisfaction on the part of both students and faculty. The most positive responses arose from the sense of a unified approach to learning and teaching. This sense resulted as much from the perception that the faculty were consulting and working together as from the choice of themes for each unit. It was also plain that students felt a sense of membership in something exclusive--for good or bad they were all in it together.

The least satisfactory feature was the length of the commitment to the program. Thirty-six hours were clearly too many (a fact we had discovered from the attrition at the close of the first year).

We also discovered that effecting change in the University was to be a very deliberate process. Neither faculty advisors nor service agencies of the University, particularly the Registrar, adapt very well to change. While there was a carefully negotiated agreement in advance that the Integrated Humanities courses would be equivalent to many basic and area requirements, equivalents are often suspect. Many advisors were still looking for "the real thing" listed on the transcripts as "English" or "Speech." Failing to find those particular categories, they often added them to the student's program before discovering what was included in the Humanities Program. Most of the early questions of this type were answered when the director and the chairmen of the participating departments prepared lists of equivalents for advisors, the Registrar, and the Counseling Center. In fact, this practice continues. It keeps the record straight and tends to remind people in critical positions of the Program.

During the early stages, the Registrar tended to assign all Humanities credits either to area requirements or to electives. This process required waivers from the English, History, and Communication Departments that the students had filled basic University requirements in composition, speech, and western civilization.

When the University catalogue was revised to include a statement to this effect, many local and transfer problems were resolved.

Two years of the pilot project taught us some important lessons about integrating course content and about implementing a new program. If these lessons can be generalized, it is that most parts of the system, regardless of how willing they are to participate, have their limits. For instance, the desire to cooperate on the part of the faculty was always high and grew more so as they learned to work together and anticipate each other. Nevertheless, each needed some share of autonomy, especially in selecting texts and assigning grades. They were willing to agree to the themes and the schedule for presenting them, but they always insisted on having a major part in deciding which texts were the best illustration of a theme.

This was not, frankly, exactly what had been planned. The original intent was that some works might do double service in literature and history or speech and logic. Occasionally, texts were shared, but the feeling remains that certain works are most effective for certain teachers; although others might be as relevant, they lacked the confidence of the teacher.

Something similar happened with grades. While the faculty agreed to the effects of averaging, there was no consensus that one component, say literature, could really produce the same experience as another, say history, in any significant depth. This was true even between American and British literature. Each teacher knew the quality of work each student was capable of doing as far as his specialty was concerned. Teachers wanted neither to assess the work assigned by others nor to have their assignments assessed.

On the other hand, there was a sincere willingness to be guided by the Program as to when themes should appear in the sequence and what the goals and objectives of the units should be. No one seemed to be at cross purposes about the aims for values of the Program. While the historian often struggled to maintain a coherent sequence, he made a great many modifications from the traditional syllabus of the western civilization course. (For a detailed account, see "The Role of History in Integrated Humanities," Network News Exchange, 4 (1979), 17.)

Service agencies, advisors, counselors, registrars,

and assistant deans are also quick to reach their limits in interpreting requirements. As has been mentioned earlier, they have a strong tendency to follow the catalogue or only certain parts of it. While the University Bulletin gives authority to the equivalencies of the Humanities Program, not every advisor knows about us or fully trusted the catalogue. We learned another valuable lesson about public relations. Every separate agency with a role in approving a student's program or recording his progress must be kept constantly informed of what has been approved. Such information is seldom communicated from agency to agency.

Probably the most gratifying finding was that students really like integration. They like to know that several teachers are headed in the same direction and have the same subject in mind at the same time. They also have benefited from the fact that a substantial part of the faculty demands on their time has been coordinated.

But students, too, have their limits. As has been mentioned, they will submit to requirements and take recommendations for a course or two beyond the requirements, but a sense of irrelevance sets in quickly. The pilot project clearly contained too many hours or at least too much commitment, especially for entering freshmen. We never repeated the sophomore year.

The first two years proved that teachers could cooperate and in many ways could change both their approach and their way of looking at their fields. Integration is not only possible if the right material is integrated intelligently but sometimes preferable. The experience proved that students perceive a real benefit from integration, and later studies have shown that their knowledge and skills are at least equal to those of students who enrolled in more traditional courses.

One unanticipated advantage that arises from a thematic approach with team teaching is the amount of variety that can be achieved. This results in one way because each teacher has something different to contribute. What may be a secondary consideration for one may be much more crucial to another and often much more interesting to the students. In general, the quotient of tedium is reduced.

Other kinds of variety are also possible. The team teaching permits varying the class size and methods of delivery. One person may address the entire class,

114

or two may break it up into smaller discussion or recitation sections. Literature and history, which lend themselves to lectures, can be supplemented with composition, which does not.

Greater variety is also possible for the faculty. While all of the teachers are required for some sessions, at other times they can be released for other activities. Instead of meeting the same group three or four times a week for the entire semester, a teacher may be off for a week or meet with the class only once. This also produces some efficiencies in the use of faculty time and releases the faculty from some of the drudgery.

It is necessary to emphasize that from the outset, the Integrated Humanities Program was conceived to fulfill already existing requirements. This is an extremely important feature. The intention has been to present the same substantive material as traditional courses only in a different way and in a different context. Neither the University requirements nor the substance of the courses integrated into the program has been changed, and the students cover the same or similar ground. This explains the continual reference here to equivalents, which everyone, including transfer institutions, can be made to understand.

This feature became clearer to us at the end of the two years than it may have been at the beginning. The students who left after the freshman year gave us strong hints that since they had completed both the freshman English and western civilization requirements and lacked only speech, the second year was less appealing to them.

The importance of substantive content also became clearer as we investigated other programs and as we defended ours before local committees charged with approving new courses and degrees. Instead of creating new "disciplines" segregated from the mainstream of University offerings which gathered to themselves material that others were neglecting, we chose solid and often traditional works and activities.

This feature is not often very well understood. Humanities programs, whatever their focus, are generally perceived to treat only with esoteric subjects relevant only to the "Humanities" or to other categories which provide the focus. Thus, "The Cultural Components of Rural America" must, the argument goes, deal with matters found only in rural America and nowhere else. Far too frequently we have been criticized for duplicating courses already being taught. "What," someone asked once, "does Paradise Lost have to do with South Dakota?"

It is necessary constantly to correct such narrow views if integrated studies are going to produce any changes in the way universities structure their offerings. It must become axiomatic that any worthwhile undertaking has application in many contexts. The focus of our courses is regional, and whatever informs the culture of our region is valuable as it also informs the culture of other regions. Any other view relegates integrated studies to a kind of backwater and consigns their content to trivia.

Further development of the Integrated Humanities Program began in the spring of 1977 with further assistance from the National Endowment for the Humanities. Based on our findings and conclusions from the pilot project, we began development of a program with two levels--one for freshmen and one for upper-division and graduate students.

During the summers of 1977 and 1978, sixteen faculty members from Art, Classics, Communication, English, History, Modern Languages, Political Science, Philosophy, Biology, and Physics were given stipends to redesign the freshman classes and develop eight separate upper-level courses combining two or more disciplines based on regional issues.

The freshman program, Humanities 101/102, still entitled "The Cultural Components of Rural America," presently comprises 18 semester hours, nine each semester. These courses are equivalent to freshman English, western civilization, introduction to speech, and introduction to philosophy. They fulfill all of the basic requirements in English, history, and speech and provide three hours of any area requirements in the Humanities.

Each semester, three or four of the themes listed on pages 109-110 are chosen as the basis for lectures and discussions and for reading, writing, and speaking assignments. The Departments of English, Classics, and Modern Languages supply three teachers for literature and composition (but not for second languages which are taught entirely separately from the Program). History provides western civilization; Communication, speech; and Philosophy, ethics and logic.

This arrangement requires six teachers each semester. Each is entirely responsible for certain parts of the course and for certain times during the week. Other parts are shared, especially the discussion sessions and the composition and speech components. The purpose here is to provide considerable freedom in selecting materials and in grading but not such complete autonomy that the course breaks down into six separate sections. For example, literature lectures and discussions are held in plenary sessions and the duties are shared by all three teachers from Classics, English, and Modern Languages. The composition sections, however, meet separately and each of these same teachers is assigned one-third of the students for composition for the entire semester.

One feature that the course has introduced at the University is assigning written composition to faculty from departments other than English--namely Classics and Modern Languages. This has worked out very well without becoming a threat either to the members of the English or languages faculties. Under the leadership of the representatives of the English Department, the composition teachers select texts and set general objectives. The individual nature of composition precluded much more direction than friendly advice, so that while students receive a consistent and coherent course in writing, they also receive a variety of points of view and approaches to literature.

The advanced program was originally intended to be made up of eight courses combining the disciplines in the Humanities Division with each other or with fine arts or one of the social or natural sciences. The advanced program was to be a test of two principles: 1) whether integrating related material could provide worthwhile new avenues of learning and 2) whether courses could integrate disciplines both in and outside of the Humanities without essential loss of quality to any participating discipline.

The original list of courses included these.

"Art, Literature, and the American Land," combining art history and American literature,
"The Immigrant Experience," combining American and European literature,
"Ethnic Diversity," combining sociology and American history,
"Technology and Values," combining philosophy and physics,

"The Influence of Communication Technologies,"
combining mass communications and public
address,
"Local Politics and Literature," combining American literature and political science,
"Biomedical Ethics," combining philosophy and
biology,
"The Oral Tradition," combining classics, European,
Medieval, and American Indian literature.

A ninth course, "Environmental Ethics," which had previously been approved, fit the pattern of the other
advanced courses and was added.

The faculty used the summers of 1977 and 1978 to
plan and develop these courses. Two were to be offered
each semester and, once each had been offered, were to
be combined into a minor in Integrated Humanities in
the B.A. and B.S. degrees.

Some of these intentions have been carried out; a
number of others are still in the process; others have
been dropped. As the courses were introduced into the
curriculum and throughout the period of their first
offering to the students, we gathered more information
about integrated courses at all levels of the University.

One fact which became almost immediately apparent
was that both students and their advisors needed almost
constant assurance that new courses, especially integrated courses, would not in some way increase graduation requirements. We had again underestimated the
importance of public information. While the same
principle regarding substance applied to the advanced
as to the freshman courses, both students and their
advisors were unwilling to take any risks when graduation requirements were concerned. The enrollment in
some courses upon their first offering was disappoint-
ing. Only when the participating departments made an
effort to urge the value and relevance of the integrated
courses did they do well.

Secondly, most, but not all of the courses were a
successful mix of disciplines or of teaching styles.
"Environmental Ethics," "Biomedical Ethics," "Technology and Values," "Art, Literature, and the American
Land," "Ethic Diversity," and "The Influences of
Communication Technologies" did well. They attracted
from 10 to 25 students on the first attempt and the
same or greater numbers on the second. Evaluations

held at the end of each course suggested that the students understood the aims and content of the courses and, at least as important, how the courses benefited them.

One feature which contributed to the students' attitude toward the courses was the effect of the blend of the teachers' styles, a factor over which there will never be much control. It is possible to prevent assigning obvious enemies to a teaching team, but much more difficult to determine positive traits. It is unclear how much a happy combination of personalities contributed to the continuation of some courses and, in its absence, an elimination of others.

In some instances, both of the assumptions about integrated courses underlying the design of the advanced courses proved true; in others they did not. The difference seems to lie in the nature of the disciplines combined in the courses and in the treatment of the themes upon which the courses were organized. Some disciplines--art, history, literature, and sociology--tend to reinforce each other because they have large areas of common matter but very different scholarly methods and critical approaches.

Other disciplines--the natural sciences and philosopy--can produce effective combinations for entirely opposite reasons. They have common approaches and techniques but may treat with quite different subjects. Courses combining ethics, logic, and values with technical or scientific matter were also effective.

What turned out to be less workable were combinations which were merely bland, which produced no tension arising from differences. The result was a loss of efficiency.

These results seem to indicate that new types of learning experiences will most likely result if there is some sort of tension arising from differences either in subject matter or technique.

Before we could settle on the six or so courses that we knew might be effective, we had to obtain the approval of a number of local committees and administrative agencies, including the South Dakota Regents of Higher Education. While much of this process is of only local concern, some questions have wider relevance because they stem from the nature of integrated courses and the way in which they are perceived.

Both local committees and state agencies have never completely been convinced that the integrated courses were not duplications of previously authorized courses. Objections similar to those of the freshman program were raised--how some courses were relevant to the regional focus of the program and how the combined material was different from what was being presented separately.

The best example of a course which gathered both of these objections was "Biomedical Ethics." The reviewers needed to be convinced, first, of what the course had to do with the region. The implication was that the same sociology, physiology, and philosophy would be taught in any course whether it had regional implications or not. Our response was based on the fact that the region has unique implications for decisions regarding medical care and its delivery. In short, the region is a factor, sometimes a determining one, in achieving uniqueness.

The other objection was easier to meet. While the sciences as separate courses may be quite similar to those in an integrated course, the result is very different when they are combined with what the Philosophy Departments calls "applied ethics." The sciences, which provide technological answers to questions about medicine, lend substance to ethical questions, and ethics materially changes the questions asked by scientists. It can be argued that these disciplines produce a very different course when they are combined.

A thorough discussion of administrative practices in the Program would be a study in itself. Directors of integrated studies programs occupy an administrative no-man's-land. While there may be large amounts of money involved, the lines of authority can frequently be very vague. For example, since 1975, the Program has spent over $500,000 when both the Federal and the University contributions are combined; yet we never became a distinct part of the administrative organization of the University.

This situation arises partly from the way the University views administration and partly from the nature of the Integrated Humanities Program. Because of the quota system for administrators under formula budgeting, no new program deserves an administrator because it has not earned the right to one by means of enrollments. Until the enrollments justify an administrative position (or if the enrollment is deliberately

limited), someone whose primary assignment lies elsewhere will be designated as the director. Since, from
the outset, we expected no more than 150 total students,
an additional administrative position or portion of a
position was precluded.

However, even when a director was appointed from
the teaching ranks more or less "without portfolio,"
there was no place in the administrative structure of
the University for the Program. Since instruction has
been supplied from faculty tenured in more than one
college--Arts and Sciences and Fine Arts--no single
dean has complete authority. Logically, the Program
belongs under the direct authority of the Vice President
for Academic Affairs, but, again, the enrollments hardly
justify more than passing attention from that office.

The answer has been to work out an administrative
mode in which the director becomes primarily a coor-
dinator, dealing directly with the participating deans
for instruction and with the registrar, the business
office, and the physical plant for scheduling, classrooms, reports, media services, and bookkeeping. This
lack of a central authority has its advantages in
providing considerable freedom for the director to
solve unique problems. The major disadvantage is that
there is none of the assurance of a continuing commitment to provide services as might result from departmental or division status.

The strength of the Integrated Humanities Program
lies entirely with the participating departments, and
they have found it beneficial to their interests. All
have made adjustments in their requirements and in
their individual offerings to accommodate the demands
both for instruction and for assigning credits. Again,
the fact that integrated courses are equivalent to
regular courses has been extremely beneficial to the
Program. If a course or two must be suspended or a
teacher reassigned, the returns have more than made up
for the changes.

The participating departments have benefited in
different ways. For instance, the English Department
is relieved of six sections of composition per semester
because Classics and Modern Languages have taken over
the instruction of some of that component of the Program. Likewise, Communication and History are relieved
of approximately 60 students from Introduction to Speech
and Western Civilization respectively. On the other
hand, Classics, Philosophy, and Modern Languages, which

are slightly overstaffed compared to their enrollments, can add approximately 1/3 of a position to their efforts because of their participation. This is a significant improvement in efficiency in the use of faculty time. For the first time, some departments can supply instructional assistance in some courses for which other departments are oversubscribed.

Yearly evaluations and a study prepared in anticipation of developing an integrated core curriculum have indicated some of what the students think. The more subjective results were that the Program both for freshmen and for advanced students was more demanding than regular courses but also more rewarding. While many felt themselves at first to be uneasy with the material introduced from disciplines with which they were usually unfamiliar, they were also compensated by the fact that the content was limited and focused on separate issues. They also recognized the same sense of community that the pilot group had felt. They also believed that both the teachers and the director were interested in their welfare, resulting in a slightly easier transition to new surroundings or to new areas.

Quantitative data, especially grades, have been gathered for those who completed the freshman courses from 1976 through 1979. They indicate a higher, but only slightly higher, cumulative grade point in comparison with students from traditional courses. Those who changed fields or selected a major in one of the departments participating in the Program make up a more signficiant number although many factors besides the Program have influenced their choices. Roughly 1/3 of the students taking Integrated Humanities courses chose degree programs in or related to the participating departments. About half of those transferred from their first choices; the other half were general students who were undecided at first.

Finally, those students who continued in professional programs in the schools of business and education discovered a slight advantage in fulfilling basic requirements. They were able to complete general requirements for English, speech, and the social sciences approximately one semester earlier.

The Integrated Humanities Program at the present time consists of two nine semester hour freshman courses for approximately 60 students providing credit in freshman English, western civilization, speech, and philosophy. The advanced courses provide a total of eighteen semester hours in six separate integrated courses covering literature, art, philosophy, and the social and natural sciences. A seminar course, "Special Topics," has been added to act as a unifying common course for students seeking the minor.

The role of the director has evolved into that of a negotiator between the participating departments, their respective schools or colleges, and the service agencies. He or she sees that schedules are prepared, texts ordered, times and classrooms assigned, and grades recorded. All of the other administrative functions such as budgets, teaching assignments, positions, and personnel matters are carried out by the home divisions of the participating faculty.

The future of both parts of the Program is as certain as the future of any course of study can be under current conditions. Fiscal and enrollment pressures will, no doubt, produce changes in the future shape of the Program as they have before. Presently the enthusiasm of the students and the determination of the participating departments is sufficient for the immediate future.

Finally, the Integrated Humanities Program has fostered other projects in the Humanities. One, "The Extended Teacher Institutes," provides an opportunity for high school teachers from the region to study the freshman courses and to develop integrated courses which apply to conditions in their own schools and local communities. Two summers were devoted to developing integrated courses in approximately 20 area high schools.

If the present courses are maintained or expanded, we shall have moved much closer to the objectives for revitalizing the Humanities and increasing their role in undergraduate education begun in 1975.

Stephen H. Dill
Department of English

124

EXTENDED TEACHER INSTITUTES
UNIVERSITY OF SOUTH DAKOTA

The Integrated Humanities Program, "The Cultural Components of Rural America," begun at the University of South Dakota in 1975, has since been the stimulus for several important curricular revisions and innovations. Prominent among these is a series of intensive summer workshops for high school teachers, the Extended Teacher Institutes, supported by the National Endowment for the Humanities. Designed to bring high school teachers together for the purpose of planning integrated humanities courses for their own schools, the Institutes provide instruction in humanities disciplines as well as practice in unit development and in the teaching of communication skills.

Prompted by the early successes of the freshman program, its director in 1978 conceived of the idea of a summer institute to prepare similar programs for introduction at the secondary level. The existing freshman program would provide a reliable working model, a point of departure for further study and eventual adaptation to an individual school's perceived needs. The proposed institute would also focus attention on the advantages of interdisciplinary efforts in approaching the teaching of humanities and would encourage the coordination of teaching plans and schedules to facilitate new ventures in humanities areas.

A preliminary survey of regional high schools indicated a substantial interest in a summer institute for the development of new courses or for the revamping of existing ones. Moreover, the survey also pointed to a willingness on the part of school administrators to contribute the requisite time, money, and facilities to such an undertaking. It was explained that teachers accepted into the program would receive a stipend, a part of which would be contributed by the local school district. Furthermore, all participants would be asked to attend two one-day workshops during the academic year, at least one of which would be hosted by one of the high schools in the program. Since these workshops would probably fall on school days, teachers also needed assurance of a release time arrangement.

The first Extended Teacher Institute was scheduled during the summer of 1980; a second was held in 1981. Each was concurrent with the university's summer school, meeting four days a week for eight weeks. Participating teachers were considered full-time students and received nine hours of graduate credit for their work. Faculty members from the university's College of Arts and Sciences and School of Education--representing the departments of English, history, physics, philosophy, communication, and curriculum and instruction--were selected because of their experiences in interdisciplinary instruction and their special interests in secondary education.

Enrollment in the Institutes were restricted for several reasons. First, since a nominal stipend was offered to participants, the number of acceptances was necessarily limited--the budget allowed for approximately thirty-five enrollments each summer. High school teachers from outside the traditional humanities areas (e.g. the sciences and certain social sciences) were acceptable, but only if their teaching normally includes humanities content--a consideration of their subject as it relates to the human condition and discussion of questions of values thus raised. Finally, since the organizing principle of the Institutes was a regional focus, narrowed now from the "Rural America" concept of the freshman program to the more immediate Upper Great Plains area, application was limited to teachers in the four-state region which includes Iowa, Minnesota, Nebraska, and South Dakota.

Interested individuals applied and were accepted by school teams. Each team was to include at least two and no more than five classroom teachers and at least one administrator whose normal responsibilities include curriculum supervision and class scheduling. Although the administrator was required to attend during only two weeks of the session, his or her participation was considered an essential part of the program. Not only would the administrator be in a position to coordinate planning and teaching activities within each school, but that person could also play a crucial role as a liaison between the teachers, their proposed humanities program, and members of the higher administration, including the school board. Administrators in the first two Institutes have been curriculum directors, assistant principals, principals, and superintendents, and their advocacy of humanities programming has in several cases proved to be the deciding factor in effecting proposed curricular changes.

It was suggested in publicity materials that each team include among its members at least one English teacher and one teacher from a social studies area, preferably history. Traditionally, literature and history have been closely allied at the high school level, and we reasoned that teachers from these areas would in most cases be at the core of any eventual humanities program. In the Institutes of 1980 and 1981, of the fifty-three teachers and thirteen administrators who attended, most were, in fact, English and history teachers. A great variety of other areas were represented, however, including government, languages, speech, art, biology, chemistry, and library science. Since small schools are characteristic of the Upper Great Plains states, it is not unusual to find teachers assigned to two, three, or even four different subject areas. Considering secondary assignments, therefore, the Institutes have also included teachers of mathematics, business, home economics, physical education, as well as several debate coaches and athletic coaches.

Each summer Institute consisted of three separate but coordinated courses, each of which was scheduled to meet every day during the term. Central to the purpose of the Institute was a general humanities or "content" class which provided instruction in literature, history, science, and philosophy. The second course focussed on the teaching of effective communication skills, especially speaking and writing. The third class was a methods practicum which allowed participants the opportunity to study interdisciplinary and team teaching. It also required the teams present to begin preparation of actual teaching units for their own schools.

The single greatest problem encountered in the realization of the Institutes concerned organization. The heterogeneity of the participants precluded any orthodox approach. This was especially true for the general humanities class. How, for example, can one present literature or history to a class which includes both those with advanced degrees in the particular area as well as individuals whose background is minimal? Furthermore, how can the disciplines of literature and history be combined with science and philosophy to form a single unit of learning?

One answer to both questions was thematic organization. Under the general heading of "Upper Great Plains Studies," the instructors themselves chose four themes as points of concentration and coordination. The role of each faculty member was then to illustrate what his or her own discipline might contribute to the elucidation of those themes. Each faculty member could select appropriate reading materials, and each was allotted time during each week for presentation. Careful planning for selection of materials as well as frequent discussions of intended teaching directions and strategies was essential. Furthermore, to ensure a common purpose and direction, all faculty members were present during all the class periods, and they were encouraged to enter into general class discussions when appropriate and to draw parallels in their own presentations when possible.

During the 1981 Institute, the organizational themes were: 1) The Immigrant Experience, 2) Social Change, 3) The Impact of Technology, and 4) Aesthetic Expression. Each scheduled to fill a two-week teaching period. During the first segment, for example, the history professor presented the background of immigration to the New World and the Upper Great Plains, and he discussed the consequent regional effects of religious pluralism. The literature teacher asked the group to read Willa Cather's My Antonia, concentrating particularly on the "Garden of Eden" and "Sense of Community" motifs. The scientist described theories and practice of terraforming and raised the question of possible future emigration into space. The philosophy teacher concentrated on cultural and social values systems, with particular reference to Native American societies.

The other three themes were approached in a similar fashion. A good deal of time was reserved for discussions, and guest speakers from various areas of the university were invited to make special contributions as warranted. Although no theme was or could be totally explored in such an abbreviated time span, the presentations were quite satisfactory to illustrate what can be done to bring several teaching disciplines together in a coordinated and cohesive learning experience.

The "skills" class was developed to stress the importance of teaching verbal communication skills throughout the curriculum. Obviously, speech and English classes are traditional sources of instruction in this area. Teachers in other fields may assume a greater or lesser degree of responsibility for teaching verbal skills or, as often happens, they may neglect this function entirely. One of the major goals of the Institutes was to impress upon the participants the advantages of a team effort in building effective communication skills.

128

A variety of exercises helped all Institute participants, whatever their teaching field, to become involved in demonstration and evaluation of verbal work. Teams devised ways to cooperate in assigning communication activities as well as means to stress meaningful substance and good form simultaneously. Participants experimented with and responded to policy debates, role playing, patterned discussions, audio-visual stimuli, and team-taught lessons. The required work for this part of the Institute included several written assignments which were consequently evaluated by at least two faculty members, one reading primarily for content and another for form and style. Most of these assignments were made jointly with faculty from the "content" class, which served to coordinate the work being done and also to economize on the amount of work expected. Through this class, teachers from all subjects of the high school curriculum profited from ideas and tactics already developed by their colleagues in English and speech. But most importantly, they became aware of what can be accomplished when the teaching of skills becomes a subject-oriented part of the total curriculum.

The third part of the Institute, the "methods" class, was taught by personnel from the School of Education who know the high schools in the region, who are cognizant of the strengths and limitations in those schools, and who are themselves experienced in secondary curriculum development. During this part of the summer program, teams were able to work together in formulating a plan for their own home schools and to prepare actual teaching units using the same four general themes being elucidated in the "content" class. On a rotating basis, both humanities and education faculty members worked with each team, assisting team members in the planning of methods and materials. By the end of the summer sessions, each group had developed several teaching units which are intended to become a part of a humanities program in their own schools.

It is perhaps beneficial to mention the testing and grading procedures we applied, since any interdisciplinary program of this nature will inevitably encounter those questions. In our case, individual freedom was the most workable arrangement. A total of nine faculty members were involved in instruction, with specific assignment to one of the three courses being offered. Instructors made assignments and tested as they deemed appropriate, keeping in mind, of course, that their own contribution represented only a fraction (actually from one-half to one-fourth) of the whole class as it was being taught. It was the director's responsibility to assure that the students' workload did not become excessive simply because of the number of faculty involved. Final grades, it was agreed, would be assigned by each faculty member, and the director would construct the average marks for each student. This system, simple and straightforward, proved to be entirely satisfactory for our purposes.

According to our original intentions, each summer Institute is really only the first step of a long-range project. Each team is expected to spend the subsequent school year in a continuing-planning phase. Teachers need more than an eight-week Institute to develop new courses and programs--unit sketches require further detailed work, other teachers in the home school need to be enlisted to the effort, school boards must consider proposals, schedules have to be worked out, and some recruiting of students must take place. Program changes in area high schools resulting from the 1980 Institute will thus be effected in the fall of 1981 at the earliest, and the 1981 summer group will continue to plan throughout 1981-82, with new programs inaugurated in the fall of 1982. Meanwhile, to keep initiative alive, two one-day workshops are scheduled during each academic year, and faculty members make periodic on-site visits to participating schools.

At the time of this writing, the Extended Teacher Institute project is progressing according to schedule. Two summer programs have been completed, accommodating a total of sixty-six individuals who represent sixteen schools in the Upper Great Plains regions. By all indications, new high school programs are getting under way with the new academic year, some are slated to begin during the second semester, and several major modifications have been accomplished, all the outcome of the 1980 Institute. Teams which have recently completed the 1981 summer program are now only at the beginning of the continuing-planning phase.

NEH support for the project will terminate in April, 1982. Plans for a third summer program are still uncertain, pending results of the formal evaluation of the entire project which is now under way. A change in funding sources, however, will necessarily entail some rather fundamental changes in organization and procedures. What those changes will be are not yet clear.

The original goal of the Extended Teacher Institutes, that of preparing interdisciplinary humanities courses for secondary schools, seems to have been successfully met. As a result of the project, a large number of high school students in the Upper Great Plains region may come to know the benefits of integrative learning and consequently may better understand the humanities and their application to our daily lives.

Gale Crouse
Department of Modern Languages

132

SELECTED BIBLIOGRAPHY

Adelson, Marvin, "Creativity and the Third Culture: A University-Level Problem," UCLA Educator, 18 (Spr. 76), 40-49.   An integrative, practical approach to both liberal learning and professional preparation.

Ashdown, Ellen A., "Humaniteis Textbook Publishers Compete for Changing Market," Humanities Report (July 80), 9-11.   An analysis of some of the solutions by textbook publishers of the problems of providing academically credible textbooks in the face of the widely varying demands of teachers of humanities courses.

Austenson, Roy A., "History and the Humanities: An Integrative Approach," Social Studies, 66 (Sep./Oct. 74), 210-14.   An alternative to the survey approach for teaching history in which history is integrated with art, music, and literature.

Babb, Lawrence A., "Interdisciplinary Studies: Proceed With Caution," Independent School, 38 (May 79), 23-27.   Interdisciplinary work as part of a larger pattern in which the disciplines as such must occupy a central position.

Bailey, Howard R., "The S-90 Series: An Approach to Creativity, Flexibility, and Relevance," Improving College and University Teaching, 23 (Sum. 75), 143-44.   A block of five courses in each department of Pershing College; a successful plan for a small college with limited faculty.

Belford, Jules, "A Model for the Development of an Undergraduate Humanities Program," Improving College and University Teaching, 27 (Spr. 79), 88-92.   A model for the development of an undergraduate humanities program with an integrated curriculum that critically examines the international heritage of the U.S. and also addresses current needs.

Binder, Arnold et al., "Social Ecology: An Emerging Multidiscipline," Journal of Environmental Education, 7 (75), 32-43.   The theoretical bases of a university social ecology program expressed in biology, sociology, and psychology emphasizing man as a biological organism interacting in a cultural-physical environment.

Bostock, William, "The Boundary Between Languages and the Social Sciences," Babel: Journal of the Australian Federation of Modern Language Teachers' Associations, 11 (Apr. 74), 14-18.   Isolation of language study from other disciplines in Australia; the desirability of integration of foreign language and social study.

Brenneke, Judith Staley and Soper, John C., "Economic Education: A Going Concern," Balance Sheet, 61 (Oct. 79), 64-67.   Describes interdisciplinary training programs for teachers in K-14 schools provided by state councils and college centers for economic education.

Bridger, J.D.F., "An Interdisciplinary Curriculum Linking Geology with Prehistoric Archaeology," Journal of Geological Education, 27 (Sep. 79), 160-61. The interdisciplinary curriculum of the Hull College of Higher Education especially a course entitled "Evolution and Prehistory."

Brillhart, L. and Debs, M.B., "Team Teaching and Faculty Development: A Simultaneous Process," Educational Research and Methods, 2 (79), 18-20.   The increasing awareness of the need for an interdisciplinary approach to science and the humanities and the necessary steps to establish a team-taught English course for engineering students.

Brock, D. Heyward, "Program in the Culture of Biomedicine at the University of Delaware," Liberal Education, 65 (Spr. 79), 92-97.   An interdisciplinary program providing a humanistically-oriented education for preprofessional students, particularly those in the health sciences.

Brownell, Judith, "Elwood Murray's Interdisciplinary Analogue Laboratory," Communication Education, 28 (Jan. 79), 9-21.   Describes Elwood Murray's interdisciplinary analogue laboratory which was designed to identify analogous structures occurring in different fields of education.

Burtin, Orville Vernon, "Using the Computer and Manuscript Census Returns to Teach American Social History," History Teacher, 13 (Nov. 79), 71-88. An undergraduate course in which students analyze census returns by means of computer and present papers to other students and faculty.

Cahn, Steven M., ed. Scholars Who Teach: The Art of College Teaching. New York: Nelson-Hall, 1978.

Cantor, Harold, "Reintegrating the Humanities," Change, 10 (Oct. 78), 54-5. Examples of current approaches by two-year colleges to integrated humanities or interdisciplinary courses.

Carrithers, Gale H., Jr., "The Two Cities and the Framing Questions," ADE Bulletin, 62 (Sep./Nov. 79), 88-94. Encourages English department chairpersons to adopt a cross-disciplinary approach and suggests a sequence of cross-disciplinary courses.

Cassidy, Harold G., "A Natural Philosophy Course in Physics and Chemistry," Journal of Chemical Education, 46 (Feb. 69), 64-66.

Cook, E.E., "An Engineering Educator's Experience in Interdisciplinary Team Teaching," Engineering Education, 65 (Dec. 74), 230-32. Describes a program designed to answer the emotionalism and sensationalism propounded by the broad spectrum ecologist.

Cotterrell, Roger B.M., "Interdisciplinarity: The Expansion of Knowledge and the Design of Research," Higher Education Review, 11 (Sum. 79), 47-56. The opportunities for new applications of existing resources and for reorganization of educational institutions in interdisciplinary research.

Cowell, Raymond. Critical Enterprise: English Studies in Higher Education. London: Allen and Unwin, 1975.

"Dialog: Is a Core Curriculum the Best Way to Educate Students to Deal with the Future?" Change, March, 1979, pp. 26-28.

Dill, Stephen H., "The Role of History in the Integrated Humanities Program," Network News Exchange, 4 (Fall 79), 16-17. Describes the part played by history in a thematically based humanities course and the problems the thematic arrangement creates for the history teacher.

Doebler, Bettie Anne, "Skinning Cats and Interdisci-

plinary Studies: A Cavaet." Change (Nov./Dec. 80),
pp. 10-12.

Duncan W. Jack, "Professional Education and the Liber-
ating Tradition: An Action Alternative," Liberal
Education, 43 (Oct. 77), 453-61.   A plan for
incorporating more humanistic concerns into professional education.

Eckhardt, Caroling D. Interdisciplinary Programs and
Administrative Structures: Problems and Prospects
for the 80s. University Park (Penn.): Pennsylvania State University Press, 1978.

Edington, W.F. and Preville, E.J., "A Journey Toward
Unity," Engineering Education, 65 (Dec. 74), 213-
15.   Traces the integration of engineering, humanities, and social sciences from the major
objectives of 1955 to present curricula designed
to produce the socio-engineer.

Fedo, David. A., "Learning for Careers and Life: Liberal
Arts in the Professional Institutions," College
Board Review, 105 (Fall 77), 28-33.   Examples of
interdisciplinary approaches in business and health
institutions.

Foa, Lin, "The Integrated Humanities in Higher Education: A Survey," Journal of Aesthetic Education, 7
(Jul. 73), 85-98.   An attempt to evaluate 134
humanities programs.

Foster, Susan L. and Burke, Armand, "The Fine Arts and
General Education: Are They Compatible?" Liberal
Education, 64 (Mar. 78), 55-62.   Theoretical
considerations which could resolve the conflict
between fine arts and general education curriculums; an analysis of one practical application of
these ideas; a proposed total curriculum integration.

Fulcher, James, "Liberal Education: Interdisciplinary
Study of Integrative Topics," Improving College
and University Teaching, 26 (Win. 78) 44-7.   A
liberal education program at Lincoln College.

Frederick, William C., "Education for Social Responsibility: What the Business Schools Are Doing About
It," Liberal Education, 63 (May 77), 190-203.
A new field of study, often called "Business
and Society" or "Business and its Environment."

Galie, Peter and Berlin, Barry, "Departments Take Adversary Roles in Law Course," Journalism Educator, 34 (Jan. 80), 13-16.   Description of a course on media law and ethics using a modified adversary context in a team teaching approach.

Gosselin, Edward A. and Lerner, Lawrence S., "History of Science as a Device for Reconciling the Sciences and the Humanities," Teaching History: A Journal of Methods, 2 (Fall 77), 41-9.   The rationale and course outlines for two college-level courses which integrate scientific and humanistic thought.

Grace, Richard E., "Nontraditional Engineering Programs: The Purdue Experience," Engineering Education, 70 (Dec. 79), 261-65.   Focuses on nontraditional engineering programs in American Universities with data that summarizes the enrollment trends since the 1960s at Purdue's Division of Interdisciplinary Engineering Studies.

Gudykunst, William B. et al., "An Analysis of an Integrated Approach to Cross-Cultural Training," International Journal of Inter-Cultural Relations, 1 (Sum. 77), 99-110.   Six approaches currently used for cross-cultural training noting the advantages of an "integrated" approach.

Guidry, Rosaline, "A Design for Teaching Human Behavior in a Generalist Undergraduate Program," Journal of Education for Social Work, 15 (Spr. 79), 45-50.   A design for teaching human behavior to undergraduate students in a multi-disciplinary class employing a comparative and analytical approach to theoretical concepts.

Huber, Curtis E., "The Dynamics of Change: A Core Humanities Program," Liberal Education, 63 (May 77), 159-70. Pacific Lutheran's integrated studies program of eight courses and one seminar all with "Dynamics of Change" as the theme.

Kahne, Stephen, "Introducing Systems Concepts to All University Students," Engineering Education, 70 (Feb. 80), 427-29.   An argument that systems thinking transcends disciplinary boundaries and should be part of everyone's education; the future importance of systems global models and their capacity for planning and decision making on a world scale.

Kessler, Martha Stout and Myers, Robert J., "A Curriculum in Business and Public Communication for Humanities Students," ABCA Bulletin, 43 (Mar. 80), 6-7.

Killian, C. Rodney and Warrick, Catherine M., "Steps to Abstract Reasoning: An Interdisciplinary Program for Cognitive Development," Alternative Higher Education: The Journal of Non-Traditional Studies, 4 (Spr. 80), 189-200.   A learning cycle approach to undergraduate instruction implemented in a variety of subjects at Metropolitan State College in Denver.

Kockelman's Joseph J., ed. Interdisciplinarity and Higher Education. University Park: Pennsylvania State University Press, 1979.

Kornfield, Milton, "A New Opportunity for General Education," Alternative Higher Education: The Journal of Non-Traditional Studies, 3 (Sum. 79), 254-59.   The problems associated with core curriculums and distribution requirements; team teaching structure with an interdisciplinary orientation that also considers the needs of different student populations.

Labianca, Dominick A., "A Non-Traditional Science Laboratory for the Non-Science Major," Journal of Chemical Education, 57 (Mar. 80), 198-99.   An interdisciplinary curriculum focusing on chemistry with a central theme of pollution--of the human body and its surroundings.

Laidlaw, Toni Ann and Dubinsky, Lon, "Eight Questions in Search of an Answer: Awakening Students to the Experience of Adolescence," Curriculum Inquiry, 10 (Spr. 80), 77-97.   The rationale, description, and evaluation of a course about adolescence taught to university students, with materials from literature, philosophy, history, and the arts.

Lowry, George G., "An Integrated Physics-Chemistry Curriculum for Science Majors," Journal of Chemistry Education, 46 (Jun. 69), 393-95.

Luskin, Bernard J., "A Portable Course with Pop Culture," New Directions for Community Colleges, 3 (Win. 75), 9-16.   An interdisciplinary humanities program which uses rock music, current movies, and television.

Lynch, James, "Recent Integrative Trends in Further Education in England and Wales," *International Review of Education*, 24 (1978), 177-85.   A review of some of the acts, reports, and study council actions which have impacted on further (post-compulsory) education since 1944.

McFarlane, Allan H. et al., "The Clinical Behavioral Sciences Program: Postprofessional Education in Mental Health," *Journal of Medical Education*, 55 (Jan. 80), 70-71.   The clinical behavioral sciences program at McMaster University, an interdisciplinary approach to mental health education.

Magada, Virginia and Moore, Michael, "The Humanities Cluster College at Bowling Green State University: Its Middle Years," *Liberal Education*, 62 (Mar. 76), 100-12.   An analysis of the curriculum, operation, and evaluation of the Bowling Green State University Humanities Cluster College, an interdepartmental living-learning program. Compares the 1975 program with those of earlier experimental years.

Mandel, Jerry E. and Hellweg, Susan A., "A Response to Increasing Faculty Resource Constraints: The Development of Umbrella Academic Programs and New Curricular Aggregates from Existing Instructional Resources," *Planning for Higher Education*, 7 (Jun. 79), 19-22.   Two curricular planning strategies that provide for academic growth with minimum resource proliferation.

Mayville, William V. *Interdisciplinarity: The Mutable Paradigm*. Washington: Eric Clearinghouse for the American Association for Higher Education, 1978.

Michel, Joseph, "Departmental and College Governance," *ADFL Bulletin*, 11 (Nov. 79), 25-29.   Discusses the traditional university organizational structure versus an interdisciplinary approach.

Morrison, James L. and Swora, Tamara, "Interdisciplinary and Higher Education," *Journal of General Education*, 26 (Apr. 74), 45-52.   The need for development of interdisciplinary programs.

Peterson, Roy P. and Hall, Stephen K., "Environmental Education for the Non-science Major," *Science Education*, 58 (Jan./Mar. 74), 57-63.   Discusses the need for interdisciplinary environmental edu-

cation, particularly at the level of higher and
continuing education.

Poppino, Mary A. and Cohen, Elaine L., "Coordinated
Curriculum Model for Reading in the Content Area,"
Journal of Developmental and Remedial Education,
2 (Win. 79), 5-7. A model designed to integrate curricula of a content course with a study
skills course.

Press, Harriet Baylor, "Basic Motivation for Basic
Skills: The Interdependent Approach to Interdisciplinary Writing," College English, 41 (Nov. 79),
310-13. Advocates the teaching of interdependent courses which combine a section of composition
with an introductory course in another discipline.

Ratcliffe, G., "Crossdisciplinary Courses for Polytech-
nics," Physics Education, 10 (June. 75), 272-273.
A rationale for the development of cross disciplinary courses.

Rhyner, C.R. et al., "The Chemistry-Physics Program at
the University of Wisconsin-Green Bay," American
Journal of Physics, 42 (Dec. 74), 1106-11. Presents the objectives, content structure, and administrative procedures of an integrated chemistry-
physics program.

Robbins, Larry M., "Integrating Communication Instruction in the Wharton MBA Curriculum," ABCA Bulletin,
42 (Sep. 79), 1-2. Describes the Wharton communication program which integrates writing
instruction within the graduate school's core
courses.

Romey, William D., "Problem-Centered Studies: Who is
the Integrator?" School Science and Mathematics,
75 (Jan. 75), 30-38. The basic requirements
for genuinely transdisciplinary studies; ways of
transcending the boundaries of the disciplines.

Rosenberg, Howard, "The Art of the Popular Film Adds
Depth to Multicultural Studies," Art Education,
32 (Feb. 79), 10-14. A narrative description
of a 14-week interdisciplinary course offered by
the University of Nevada, Reno.

Rosse, Cornelius, "Integrated Versus Discipline-Oriented
Instruction in Medical Education," Journal of
Medical Education, 49 (Oct. 74), 995-98.

Rudolph, Frederick. _Curriculum: A History of American Undergraduate Courses of Study Since 1636._ New York: Jossey-Bass (Carnegie Council Series), 1977.

Schacter, Steven C., "Death and Dying Education in a Medical School Curriculum," _Journal of Medical Education_, 54 (Aug. 79), 661-63. A student-initiated course on death and dying, offered at the Case Western Reserve University School of Medicine.

Singh, Yogendra, "Constraints, Contradictions and Inter-disciplinary Orientations: The Indian Context," _International Social Science Journal_, 31 (1979), 114-22. Identifies problems and contradictions which are inherent in social teaching in India in a search for indigenous theoretical models to replace models developed by colonial nations.

Spratlen, Thaddeus H., "The Educational Relevance of Black Studies--An Interdisciplinary and Inter-Cultural Interpretation," _Western Journal of Black Studies_, 1 (Mar. 77), 38-45. Interdisciplinary and intercultural aspects of Black studies programs and the educational relevance of Black studies.

Spurlock, Karla J., "Toward the Evolution of a Unitary Discipline: Maximizing the Interdisciplinary Concept in African/Afro-American Studies," _Western Journal of Black Studies_, 1 (Sep. 77), 224-28. Curricular and extracurricular strategies suggested for achieving a valuable interdisciplinary framework for Black student programs.

Squires, Geoffrey. _Interdisciplinarity_. London: The Group for Research and Innovation in Higher Education, 1975.

Taylor, Karl K., "DOORS English--The Cognitive Basis of Rhetorical Models," _Journal of Basic Writing_, 2 (Spr./Sum. 79), 52-66. The development of an interdisciplinary Operational Reasoning Skills (DOORS) Program at Illinois Central College.

Thompson, Lee, "International Environmental Problems," _International Educational and Cultural Exchange_, 7 (Sum. 71), 61-66. The planning and foreign students' evaluation of an experimental interdisciplinary course in international environmental problems.

Tovey, Duane R. and Weible, Thomas D., "Social Studies, Thought, and Language," Social Studies, 70 (Jul./Aug. 79), 167-69. Thought and language in social studies education and an Ohio State University program which integrates social studies instruction and active learning-language experiences.

Wagner, Carl and Struzynski, Antony, "On the Autonomy of Psychology in Psychology/Religion Courses: An Optimistic View," Teaching of Psychology, 6 (Oct. 79), 140-43. Affirms the possibility of interdisciplinary psychology/religion courses in which both remain autonomous.

Watkins, Ed, "Integrating the Life Development Concept into the Curriculum," New Directions for Education, Work, and Careers, 1979, 49-74. A comprehensive effort launched by Doane College in 1973 to blend the career development concept into its liberal arts framework.

Winthrop, Henry. Education and Culture in the Complex Society: Perspectives on Interdisciplinary and General Education. Tampa: University of South Florida Press, 1979.

Wooton, Lutian R., et al., "A Response to Student Needs for Knowledge and Innovations in Education," Contemporary Education, 50 (Spr. 79), 166-68. A graduate course in educational trends designed to provide an overview of educational developments through an interdisciplinary approach to curriculum innovations.

Frank R. Cunningham
Susan J. Wolfe
Department of English
University of South Dakota